The Truth About Talent

The Truth About Talent

A guide to building a dynamic workforce, realizing
potential and helping leaders succeed

Jacqueline Davies and Jeremy Kourdi

JOSSEY-BASS
A Wiley Imprint
www.josseybass.com

This edition first published in 2010
Copyright © 2010 John Wiley & Sons Ltd.

Registered office
John Wiley & Sons Ltd, The Atrium, Southern Gate, Chichester, West Sussex, PO19 8SQ,
United Kingdom

Under the Jossey-Bass imprint, 989 Market Street, San Francisco CA94103-1741, USA www.
jossey-bass.com

For details of our global editorial offices, for customer services and for information about how to
apply for permission to reuse the copyright material in this book please see our website at www.
wiley.com

Library of Congress Cataloging-in-Publication Data

Davies, Jacqueline.
   The truth about talent : a guide to building a dynamic workforce, realizing potential, and
helping leaders succeed / by Jacqueline Davies and Jeremy Kourdi.
      p. cm.
   ISBN 978-0-470-74882-4 (hardback)
   1. Employee motivation.   2. Personnel management.   3. Ability.
I. Kourdi, Jeremy. II. Title.
   HF5549.5.M63D38 2010
   658.3'14—dc22

                                                                          2010014530

A catalogue record for this book is available from the British Library.

Typeset in 10.5 on 15 pt Monotype Janson by Toppan Best-set Premedia Limited
Printed in Great Britain by TJ International Ltd., Padstow, Cornwall

This book is for our children and in particular, Alix who has recently arrived and Jacqueline's young nieces Ella and Mia. We look forward to a future where you can fulfil all of your potential at work.

Contents

Introduction

The future is a race between education and catastrophe

HG Wells

The beginning of our research for this book coincided with the greatest economic crash of our time. Curiously this brought with it a greater sense of insecurity about employment but a more vociferous set of opinions about how organizations should be led. It widened the public debate on how companies take risks and the character of executives who authorize them. Lehman collapsed, generating a tide of business foreclosures across the world. For the first time since World War II, governments stepped into the markets to prevent the financial system spiralling into disaster. Banks became publicly owned and effigies of bank executives were hanged from lamp posts in the City of London. US unemployment hit 10%, the highest rate since the 1929 Crash.

Socially, we had also entered a new era. Having enjoyed the growth in credit and in our pay packets we began to feel troubled about consumption. Carbon footprints and climate change dominated the media schedules: trying to live in a more sustainable way became a popular preoccupation. We began to understand our interdependence and connection with communities on the other side of the world, questioning how clothes could be made for only a few US cents and scrutinizing the production and employment practices of the companies who had achieved this.

Alongside this, the debate about work itself had come of age. Numerous voices in the blogosphere were asking why work was so out of date. They pointed to social changes – particularly technology-based networks and the trend towards consumer customization, and asked *'how come we don't work like this?'* We also noticed a huge proliferation of employer review sites. This is much like the citizen consumer trend, where customers review services and warn each other of poor quality or delivery. Employees were going on-line to tell each other about what their work experience was really like and to publicly rate their CEO's performance.

It was also clear from our review of talent management literature and opinion that a shift in perspective was underway. We noticed that commentators were beginning to question the effectiveness of conventional techniques and querying their return on investment. The boldest of these criticisms came from Peter Cappelli in the excellent book *Talent on Demand*, charting the rise and fall of the talent management era. Cappelli's key assertion is that today's talent management practices are from the 1950s and that the ebb and flow of the labour market requires a more dynamic approach. He proposes a just-in-time supply management approach, ensuring that companies have the talent they need when they need it. This would minimize the risk of having underutilized 'inventory', too much talent for the business to employ, or too little, with insufficient skills or vacancies limiting growth. His proposal to adopt a 'Make and Buy' strategy is, in our opinion, the most pragmatic we have seen. It requires more sophisticated forecasting and more just-in-time development offerings.

While we endorse this step forward, it felt to us that the success of these two approaches (Make and Buy) is entirely dependent on the culture, strategy and relationships of the organization they sit in. This 'systems' dimension to the talent problem is overlooked in the wider literature where commentators concentrate on increasingly sophisticated ways to find and develop 'our brightest people' and 'our future leaders'. This takes place in a Western business culture where talent is about an individual's potential to reach executive levels. This has led to a range of talent management practices all focused on selecting in (and screening out) individuals into two groups: the 'talent', and everyone else. While the rationale for this is initially compelling, 'we have a limited resources, we can only invest in those who will give us the best return on our investment', we had grown increasingly sceptical about whether this had indeed delivered the benefits it had promised.

Recognizing the talent 'doom loop'

As practitioners in this area we have both bought into this notion, and worked for many years to make it happen. We have worked with CEOs, undertaking extensive talent reviews. We have worked with psychologists assessing people's capability. We have worked with technology specialists to introduce databases to capture skills across the workforce. We have worked with 'the talent' as coaches. We have worked with recruiters to scour the market for more talent. And yet when we reflected on the difference this activity was really making we felt that it was still not enough.

That is not to say that the work we were doing wasn't useful; it was. We provided CEOs with better insight to inform their decision-making, our systems reduced administration and the individuals we worked with grew in capability. We could (and did) measure our results for each of these activities and in each area we could see an improvement. It was when we stepped back and looked at the whole picture we could see that the dynamic problem about the quality and supply of talent organizations was not fixed. Like other professionals in this area we continued to wrestle with attraction and retention, trying to resolve this with ever-greater rewards. While we could provide our 'talent' with world-class executive education, it was a continual struggle to move them on to new roles.

The struggle was systemic and success was secured only when a complex set of organization and individual factors lined up. Was the individual mobile? Did they trust their leaders enough to take the risk? Was their current business able to let them go? Was there sufficient back fill? And so on.

In truth, we had metaphorically put sticking plasters over the obvious issues without really getting to the root cause of the problem.

We spoke with our colleagues in other organizations and they too commented on the never-ending treadmill of talent reviews, succession planning, assessment and development. Many were weary with an engine of bureaucracy that had almost taken on a life of its own. Although all were busy, very few could honestly point to the commercial advantage of their talent activities. We could talk about the risks we had managed but not how our activities had contributed to our organization's long-term success. Why is it that marketing directors, product directors and finance directors become chairmen, chief executives and board members at a much, much greater rate than HR directors? Could it have something to do with a perceived lack of connection between the work of HR professionals and the direct commercial impact on the business?

It felt to us that organizations were operating in a talent 'doom loop':

The Talent Doom Loop

We believe that many organizations are now stuck in this systemic loop, with important implications for corporate governance and the pool of available talent. Two high profile CEO succession stories bring this vividly to life. Coincidentally, in February 2010 the Boards of the UK's largest retailer, Marks & Spencer, and the UK's main commercial broadcaster, ITV, announced CEO successors within the same week. Both appointments attracted much press attention, particularly since both were external candidates signed up for packages reportedly in excess of £15 million each. Coming at a time of economic difficulty, many people were naturally perplexed – not just by the eye-watering scale of the packages, but also by the fact that they appear to pay huge sums irrespective of company performance.

The justification used by both companies to defend these decisions is the limited talent available: a simple question of supply and demand. Not for the first time, this response provokes a scathing rebuke from several commentators, incredulous that such significant companies had failed to groom internal successors. What many people feel is shocking is the complete lack of succession planning and the non-suitability of any internal candidates for two of the highest profile and most commercially-significant jobs in the UK. Resigned to looking outside their organizations, both boards then discovered that the pool of senior executive talent is seemingly very small. Either UK plc has failed to develop managers capable of leading large corporations, or the boards of the biggest and best British companies just can't find them. Clearly, with the penalty for mistakes at this level running at £15 million per post, to say nothing of the problems of uncertainty and delay when replacing a CEO, this is an alarming inefficiency that surely needs to be corrected.

What seems more likely is not that great senior executives are in short supply; it's simply that boards are often completely unaware of the many neglected or underrated people who are very capable of running large, complex organizations. Because they are at the top, boards of directors get away with an unquestioning arrogance that says 'people who are capable

The practices of talent management are seriously adrift from the strategy and challenges facing organizations today.

of keeping company with us and leading this business are in incredibly short supply'. This belief is uninformed at best and potentially self-serving. It may be that there are people who can run large commercial organizations. However, they don't get an opportunity, as the directors and head-hunters prefer to opt for stars with proven track records. In other words, it is preferable to take a safety first option.

This book is our exploration of what might be happening to cause this doom loop. It is based on extensive conversations with the stakeholders and HR professionals involved in the talent system. We spoke with senior leaders and head-hunters as well as people who had been identified as 'talent' and those who hadn't. We also conducted an anonymous, global survey reaching 300 executives across Europe, the USA, South America, the Middle East, India and China. The one thing they had in common was a frustration with the way talent management was working.

About our research

The aim of our research was to understand more about the beliefs and assumptions people have about talent and how these might be influencing current practices. We used our research to return to first principles and address several questions:

- What is 'talent' and why do we need it?
- Why, even in an economic downturn, is there never enough talent?
- To what extent is talent a universal, global idea?
- How come despite the 'scarcity' of talent women and people from minority groups are still notably absent from key positions?
- Is there any relationship between the perceived talent shortage and how we see work these days?
- Who is really in control of talent?
- What are the rituals, behaviours and practices affecting the way talented people are managed?

Seven key insights

What we learned was surprising, heartening and, in places, complex. In high-level terms we learned how the practices of talent management were adrift from the strategy and challenges facing organizations today. We have summarized these into seven key insights:

1. The need to revaluate how people contribute and create value in today's economy – it is about knowledge, innovation and relationships *today* rather than executive potential tomorrow.

2. Challenging the conventional wisdom that talent refers to a 'special few' rather than the 'vital many'. Perhaps we don't have enough because we keep looking in the wrong places and doing the wrong things? *It seems counter-intuitive at best to claim that 'people are our greatest asset' and then largely neglect the talents and aspirations of the majority.*

3. Conditions facing organizations are tough and competitive and markets are turbulent. To withstand this, we need to build talented organizations *and* talented individuals.

4. Interdependence between people within and across organizations is critical. The way that each individual relies on each other and how talent is realized through social and team ties makes a decisive, defining difference.

5. Individuals control when and who their potential is shared with. The idea that an organization can manage talent and potential is an outdated conceit.

6. The nature of work itself matters hugely. The extent to which it is stimulating and engaging – and how people can make the connection with what they do and the wider difference it makes – is vital.

7. The way talent is generated is affected by the whole 'ecology' of an organization – its sense of purpose, rituals, the behaviour of its leaders, how it hires and how it fires people all influence the way talent is generated.

These observations point to a need to understand the social dimension of how talent works. We have spent so much time focused on human capital: the capability and resources that each individual offers, the *'within employee factors'* – yet we have neglected to look at the role social capital, the *'between employee factors'* plays.

How this book is organized

We have written this book to offer some ideas about breaking out of the talent doom loop. The ideas we offer are intentionally challenging. Our book is intended to stimulate new perspectives and practices. This is because the most important truths about talent are the beliefs we hold about it.

In Chapter 1: We Are All Talent Now, we start by exploding a number of the core beliefs we hold about talent. We look closely at several individual stories: Gary Flandro, a NASA summer intern, as well as Bob Woodward and Carl Bernstein, the journalists who doggedly pursued the Watergate investigation, and reflect on how they were able to make the differences that made history.

We learn that talent can come from unexpected places and that individual success is highly dependent on hard work, the timing of opportunities and the support of other colleagues. In this sense we feel it's time to more completely understand the conditions for talent; how the character of the organization shapes the way individuals perform and develop.

Chapter 2: A New Way of Thinking About Talent highlights the simple fact that to really get to grips with the idea of talent you need to understand what it is for. We look at how the changing shape of our economies is driving different needs in our organizations, and how this is influencing the demand for talent. More than ever, our organizations need to be fast, adaptable and networked. This drives the demand for a wider portfolio of talented people who, whatever their role, are able to generate sustainable value.

On the supply side there are three, significant trends that are converging: the fluctuating supply of labour, a capability crunch and more connected consumption. We look at the impact the global downturn is having on the labour market, noting that pension insecurity has postponed the predicted retirement of the Baby Boomers. Also, despite this temporary increase in the labour supply we still have a shortage of critical skills. We think that this 'capability crunch' is being caused by an education system designed more for the Industrial rather than Information Age.

Devoting all our attention to small groups of high potentials leaves our organizations dangerously exposed to changing economic conditions.

As HG Wells noted, the future is a race between education and catastrophe – and this failure to adequately prepare our children for the new world of work is the most problematic aspect of our future talent supply.

Combined with this are dynamic changes in our social lives, often brought about by technological innovation, and we find that is not reflected in our workplaces or the way we plan for talent. We explore the crucial question of 'potential for what?' and explain why devoting all our attention to small groups of high potentials leaves our organizations dangerously exposed to changing economic conditions.

Against these tremendous changes organizations will thrive by being distinctive, a fact explained in Chapter 3: Talent Diversity: You Need to Believe It to See It. Distinctiveness will be achieved through innovation and more specifically an ability to respond to the kaleidoscopic requirements of different consumer groups. Why then does the leadership of our organizations continue to look so homogenized? It is striking that despite the increased diversity in our society and our consumption (women make over 70% of purchasing decisions in the developed world and some £300 billion is spent in the UK by the combined over 55s, disabled and gay communities) this is not reflected in the leadership of our organizations. We therefore ask if our conventional methods of identifying talent are exacerbating this diversity gap.

The need for a practical, business edge to the way that people are managed and led is the subject of Chapter 4: Strategy – Beginning With the End in Mind. This chapter explains that strategy is the first priority, encompassing other tasks such as serving customers and adding value, managing finance, innovating and leading people. Strategy is a word that is, sadly, over-used and often made to appear as a 'black art' – in truth, it simply means moving a business from where it is now to where it wants to be in the future. It highlights the fact that in this essential journey the role of senior HR professionals is, surprisingly and consistently, neglected and under-valued.

A talented person is anyone that adds value to an enterprise or activity, a concept that is simultaneously simple, vital and often challenging.

The chapter also provides several practical tools enabling the business to make its strategic journey from where it is now to where it needs to be. These tools include scenario planning as well as the essentials of developing, implementing and communicating strategy. Also included in this chapter are strategic tools for HR professionals, enabling them to mobilize, stimulate and focus talented minds to move the business the right way. We have no doubt that were this to happen more, with HR professionals directly connecting what they do with the 'hard-edged' strategy and priorities of the business, we would find many more assuming the top roles of Chairman and CEO in corporations.

In Chapter 5: Hire and Wire – Developing Your Organization's Talent Ecology, we look closely at the challenge of implementing strategy. One issue that matters, but is perhaps not well understood, is the need to create the right conditions for talented people to thrive. We call this the talent ecology and it is vital if talented people are to perform. This matters because it ensures that they and their organization achieve their true potential. The forces shaping the talent ecology are explained, notably the external market conditions and the link with the organization's strategy.

As well as explaining how to manage the talent ecology we explain that a talented person is anyone who adds value to an enterprise or activity, a concept that is simultaneously simple, vital and often challenging. We also describe how best to find and nurture talent, the need to get the right structure, the importance of networks and the nature of talented teams. This chapter describes how an organization's culture can make or break their strategy. We also borrow an intelligent and highly appropriate metaphor from business writer Jim Collins, introducing the 'fly wheel effect' where small, incremental changes in an organization's culture gradually build a powerful momentum among everyone involved.

The increasingly significant issues of employer branding, the employee value proposition and segmentation are explained in Chapter 6: Getting Personal – The Workforce of One. The point here is that geographical and social mobility of labour has risen dramatically within a generation. People are concerned about themselves and their futures and they have the ability to do something with this concern. For Western employers, the concept of a career for life has largely disappeared. This has major implications for the way that people are managed. Employees need to be encouraged to bring all of their talents to work. This situation was loudly championed by business prophets like Ricardo Semler nearly two decades ago, but it has become even more urgent today. In the twenty-first century economy the time to view employees as a single 'workforce' is passing, a better approach is mass customization, viewing each individual as a workforce of one.

Meeting this challenge is no easy task. One leadership challenge is central to the task of creating value (the defining attribute of talented employees): that task is described in Chapter 7: Engaging with Talent. Employee engagement is vital to improving business performance, effectiveness and productivity. The thinking behind employee engagement is simple. If people in organizations are actively engaged with their work – not simply motivated, but valuing what they are doing and striving to do it better at all times – then they will be more productive for the organization and likely to implement the strategy, as well as being more personally fulfilled. The trick is to move from a situation where people might (or might not) be simply happy and motivated, to one where they are actively loyal, committed and engaged with their work.

In Chapter 8: The Meaning of Work we consider why people are much more than 'human resources' and why, in the future, work needs to be made much more personal and meaningful. While this is easy to say and it may sound optimistic – even naive – it is undoubtedly the case that for most employees, meaning matters. Consider, for example, the extent to which your organization succeeds with the following challenges:

- Does your organization strive to achieve positive change in society – doing things differently and better?
- Are leaders creating the right conditions for their people to develop, flourish and succeed?
- Do your company's values actually inform and guide the way people work (or are they just meaningless words)?
- Are people proud to be working for your organization?
- Are trust, energy and strong relationships commonplace?

These issues also underpin Chapter 9: Leading for Talent, which describes how the challenge of leading has been changing in recent years. Currently, some of the greatest challenges and opportunities for business leaders are posed by: greater globalization, interconnectedness and interdependence. These have led to increasing complexity and the escalating need for growth, innovation and an approach that meets rising expectations among customers and employees.

There is an answer, however, and this is explored in Chapter 10: Techniques for Realizing Talent in your Whole Workforce. This explores the connection between leadership and talent and answers several questions: how do you attract good people to your organization and how can you ensure that they achieve their full potential? How do you stimulate, engage and inspire people at all levels to achieve greatness? What practical support do people really want at work and what do they get? Above all, how can you build a dynamic workforce, help people realize their potential and enable them to succeed?

The answer to many of these leadership challenges can be found by:

- using intuition and emotional intelligence;
- applying intellect, intelligence and insight;
- showing decisive, courageous leadership and integrity.

The conclusion draws together these themes and explains how to create a system, the talent flywheel, which achieves steady, inexorable progress for the organization as well as each talented individual.

Chapter 1

We Are All Talent Now

Biologists often talk about the 'ecology' of an organism: the tallest oak in the forest is not the tallest just because it grew from the hardiest acorn: it is the tallest also because no others blocked its sunlight, the soil around it was deep and rich, no rabbit chewed through its bark as a sapling, and no lumberjack cut it down before it matured.

Malcolm Gladwell *Outliers* (Little, Brown and Company 2008)

What is talent and how is it best viewed? This chapter explains about talent and why we believe talent cannot be managed. It introduces the main issues, in particular, the belief that the context in which talent operates is as important as the individual, and the fact that engaging the whole workforce is not simply one leadership task among many, it *is* leadership. Crucially, it also explains why elite approaches to talent management don't work, and why successful businesses need to get better at realizing the potential of different types of talent across the workforce.

In the summer of 1965 Gary Flandro was a summer intern with the NASA space agency. At that time, NASA was in the middle of the first Mariner missions to Mars and Flandro was given the routine and supposedly far less interesting task of calculating, in detail, the movement and relative positions of the planets and the best time to launch a probe for a future expedition to Jupiter.

Gary Flandro approached the task carefully and enthusiastically. He understood that the gravitational field of one planet could slingshot a probe onto another target at even greater speed, and he calculated when the four largest planets in the solar system (Jupiter, Saturn, Uranus and Neptune) would be on the same side of the sun, in the same proximity. He then calculated that a specific timing for a mission to Jupiter would, because of their proximity, also enable the probe to 'slingshot' using the orbit of one of the four outer planets to visit the next and continue its journey. Finally, Gary Flandro worked out that only once every 175 years were the four planets close enough to make such a mission viable.

This was a major breakthrough in space exploration: Flandro, a Masters student on a summer internship, had discovered what has become known as the multi-planet 'Grand Tour' mission: a feat that uses gravity to enable a space craft (ultimately the Voyager) to explore the four major outer planets of the solar system. This led NASA to launch the enormously successful Pioneer and Voyager space probes that during the 1970s, 1980s and 1990s dramatically increased our understanding of the solar system. Voyager is now the most distant and far travelled object in human history and Gary Flandro's journey is also interesting. For many years, he was a professor of space exploration at the University of Tennessee and he has been named by the American Institute of Aeronautics and Astronautics among 30 of the world's finest contributors to the field of aeronautics. Not bad for a young student given a routine task to complete!

Another American of the same generation as Gary Flandro, Robert Woodward, was born in March 1943 in Illinois. He studied history and English literature at Yale University, receiving his BA degree in 1965 before beginning a five-year tour of duty in the US Navy. After being discharged as a lieutenant in August 1970 he considered attending law school but applied instead for a job as a reporter with the *Washington Post*. He was given a two-week trial but was not hired because of his lack of journalistic experience. After a year at the *Montgomery Sentinel*, a weekly newspaper in the Washington DC area, he was hired as a *Post* reporter in September, 1971. While he was at the *Washington Post* Bob Woodward was partnered with another journalist, Carl Bernstein, who had attended the University of Maryland but did not graduate. Together, these two young, relatively inexperienced journalists doggedly pursued an investigation that became the Watergate scandal, eventually resulting in the first resignation by an American president in US history when Richard Nixon resigned the presidency in August 1974.

In his 1995 memoir *A Good Life*, former executive editor of the *Washington Post* Ben Bradlee singled out Bob Woodward in the foreword, commenting that he could not overestimate the contributions made by Bob Woodward, a reporter that Bradlee viewed as the best of his generation and the best he'd ever seen. Both Woodward and Bernstein have maintained their position at the top of their profession (and, thankfully, subsequent US presidents seem to have raised their game as well).

So, what do these stories of Gary Flandro, Bob Woodward and Carl Bernstein have to do with our understanding of talent management? Several facts are quite obvious while others require a little more thought.

First, talent requires effort. It can be tempting to assume that the most talented people can do no wrong: their success seems almost preordained and all they need to do is simply 'show up'. This is not true. Gary Flandro had already graduated high school, obtained his undergraduate and master's degrees and was well on his way to obtaining his PhD. He was used to hard work and study and that, presumably, was why NASA hired him in the first place. Similarly, Woodward and Bernstein understood that their profession requires patient, diligent and sometimes tedious effort. All three worked hard. In fact, it may be misleading to call it work at all. What they did became a passion, almost certainly they were thinking constantly about the issues they faced, even when they were away from their organizations. Talent requires energy if it is to develop and flourish. Fortunately for these individuals (and the rest of us) they were able to find an area of activity – a genuine passion – that would drive them on and enable them to excel. (In his fascinating book *Outliers* the writer Malcolm Gladwell makes a similar point, providing evidence for his claim that 10,000 hours is the time required to become truly successful at a task.)

The next point about talent is that it comes from anywhere, everywhere, and can emerge at any time. For example, the administrators at NASA who hired Gary Flandro clearly believed they were getting the services of a bright college student, but they probably did not realize they were hiring one of the greatest contributors to the field of aeronautics. Similarly, Harry Rosenfeld, the *Washington Post*'s metropolitan editor who released Bob Woodward after a two-week trial in 1970, did not realize that the man with no journalistic experience who he had just let go would, within four years, have returned to the *Washington Post* and conduct an investigation leading, ultimately, to the resignation of a sitting US President.

This point – that talent comes from anywhere, everywhere, and can emerge at any time – is especially significant today, in the first decades of the twenty-first century. For the first 30 years of our lives we witnessed a world recovering from the shocks of the twentieth century. In particular, there was a Cold War, apartheid, atrocious governance, horrendous poverty in that part of the globe known as the Third World, and economic instability in the First and Second Worlds. Of course, there were many amazing successes too, especially in the fields of science and technology, but that does not obscure the fact that the late twentieth century saw huge disparities in income and opportunity around the world.

This situation now is changing. Countries such as Brazil, Russia, India and China (the 'BRIC' countries) have been developing fast, together with other populous countries dubbed the N11 (the 'Next 11' fast-developing countries after BRIC are: Bangladesh, Egypt, Indonesia, Iran, Mexico, Nigeria, Pakistan, The Philippines, South Korea, Turkey, and Vietnam; the terms 'BRIC' and 'N11' were coined by the investment bank Goldman Sachs). Moreover, the rates of economic growth are significant and sustained. For example, between 1980 and 2006 China's economy grew by an incredible 9% each year. This has helped to lift millions of people out of poverty and into an increasingly globalizing economy. Even if these fast developing countries stumble economically or politically at some point in the future, much as the Western democracies did in the first half of the twentieth century, their growth, long-term prosperity and influence now seems assured, at least during the twenty-first century. The implications of this are far reaching and they are especially significant for organizations. For example, it is a simple, sobering fact to consider that the top 5% of China's student population is significantly larger than the United Kingdom's *entire* student population.

The stories from NASA and the *Washington Post* also highlight the profound influence exerted by leaders and organizational cultures. Clearly, both organizations, NASA and the *Washington Post*, were exceptional places. Both have suffered huge setbacks and doubtless made major mistakes but, undeniably, they have come to be seen as organizations defined by the talent and character of their people and, perhaps most significantly of all, the ability to achieve their goals. Even today, the *Washington Post* is regarded as one of the world's great newspapers, while NASA still has the ability to instil excitement, awe and interest. Of course, this is in part a reflection of what they do and what they have done in the past, but, crucially, it also suggests that a whole range of leadership issues are at play when organizations enable their most talented people to develop their potential and succeed. This includes coaching and providing mutual support, team working and collaboration, innovating, building relationships and being able to develop your skills. Of course, that personal success invariably drives the organization's success, but the organization or, more specifically, the team, is driving the individual.

For example, in February 1676 Isaac Newton, the renowned British scientist, wrote to Robert Hooke, another successful scientist with whom Newton was in dispute over optical discoveries, remarking: 'If I have seen further it is by standing on the shoulders of giants'. Historians tend not to believe that this was a statement of self-effacing modesty from Newton (surely one of history's greatest ever scientists); the prevailing view is that this was instead a sarcastic attack on the curmudgeonly Hooke who, although immensely successful in his own right, was also short and hunchbacked. Whatever the true sentiment may have been behind Newton's remark, the idea has lasted throughout mathematics and science that progress is made incrementally and interdependently, by methodically building on the discoveries and insights of others. So it is with many issues in business including the need for talented people to be able to learn from what is around them and what has gone before.

Another thought that comes to mind when one reflects on the diverse stories of Flandro, Woodward and Bernstein is that these were, despite their achievements, relatively ordinary people. By their own admission these were normal individuals (at least, compared to their peers), rather than the greatest geniuses in history. Gary Flandro may have gone on to become a rocket scientist but in 1965 he was a student intern. By this we mean that it would probably not

Crucially, it is the environment in which talented people operate that allows them to develop their potential and succeed: the organization gives them access, opportunity and encouragement.

have been apparent to NASA that a summer intern would make a major contribution to the exploration of the outer planets! Similarly, no one realized that Woodward and Bernstein's investigation into a Washington DC burglary at the Watergate complex would have such far-reaching consequences. Moreover, *it almost certainly never occurred to the individuals involved.* A journalist barely out of his 20s with less than four years professional experience investigated a crime (and the high-level cover-up of that crime) bringing down a president. A student's calculations during a summer internship program were integral to the successful exploration of the outer planets. Amazing though these stories are, one suspects that most successful organizations contain many impressive but perhaps less eye-catching examples of people achieving more, and going further, than they had ever thought possible.

This is one of the most fascinating things about talent: most of us have it, or, more precisely, we are each more talented than we give ourselves credit for. The notion that we can each achieve more than we might think we call *discretionary potential* and it is one of the main themes of this book. The challenge for leaders and organizations is to find the right people and then help them to go even further than even they might have thought possible. That sounds to us like a great challenge and the meaning of great leadership.

Another insight that comes to mind when one considers the phenomena of distinctively talented employees is the fact that they always seem to display several notable characteristics. In particular, these include initiative, flexibility and drive. They display a relentless desire to find things out, to get things done and, above all, to make progress. They want to achieve things and even more than that they want their work to have *meaning.* These qualities of initiative, drive and a desire for work to have meaning have several vital implications and results. For example, they lead to passion, enthusiasm and inquisitiveness. They also propel talented employees to seek out, both consciously and, one suspects, subconsciously, new opportunities. Talented people tend to find themselves in the right place at the right time more often than other people, and that is because they are looking for opportunities, they gravitate towards them, and opportunities also come looking for them. In other words, they make their own luck.

Crucially, it is the environment in which people operate that allows them to realize their talent and succeed; who they work with, the projects they work on and how they are led. And given the shortfall in skills in today's labour market it is the task of today's leader to create an environment where the latent talents in the whole workforce can be realized.

What we mean by talent

So, what do we actually mean by '*talent*'? It is a valuable word that could become discredited with over-use or if it is used too widely without being clear about its meaning. Today, for example, we can see that 'talent' may mean someone who is physically appealing, or a Star, or a prima donna, or a capable all-rounder, or simply someone who has a specific skill. The danger is that if the term is over-used and discredited then the concepts behind it are similarly disparaged or dismissed. In business, language really does matter. For that reason we have tried to provide a very clear definition of talent: one that is grounded in business reality.

We like the conventional view that talent is a special ability or a capacity for achievement but that definition is understandably broad. When it comes to organizations and the challenges of leadership, we believe that a talented person is anyone who adds value to an enterprise or activity. Or, to put it another way, to be considered 'talent' you have to add value to something; improving it in some way.

This is one reason why talent matters so much: because it lies at the heart of improvement, innovation, competitiveness, customer service and progress. In the twenty-first century it is no longer enough simply to focus on a few 'high potential' executives, those people who demonstrate a capacity to be effective at senior levels. The twenty-first century has seen a shift towards value that results from: service/product innovation, brand experience and social relationships, and sharper insights from customers, stakeholders and wider communities.

To understand this view of talent further requires the appreciation of a simple economic truth: profitability requires scarcity. If there is an abundant supply of something (such as knowledge) then its price and value will be low. If the supply is scarce then it is more likely to be valuable and generate a profit. This is the law of supply and demand. And what is often at the root of scarcity? Skills and knowledge. For example, in the pharmaceuticals industry if there is a high demand for a product for which you have a patent and no alternative exists, the future is a lucrative one, even if the research and development costs have been substantial. In this way scarce and valuable knowledge can help deliver exceptional profits. Crucially, the source of that knowledge was people – in this case, the researchers and scientists working for the pharma company. It is important to realize, however, that it is not people, potential or talent that are scarce, it is people with the right knowledge and skills. Our organizations make life harder for themselves than they need to by ignoring the necessity for leadership, by focusing only on a chosen few, by failing to help people realize their potential, and by using the many to develop things that are original, insightful and valuable. What we need to be doing, therefore, is closing the gaps in skills. This means upgrading education and also locating business in 'talent hubs' – those places where specialist skills are in high supply.

That much may seem obvious. It is hardly a revelation that the talent in a pharma company rests with its scientists. But just as the scientist's expertise is the culmination of their background and studies and is now part of a process of generating knowledge and understanding, then producing and selling a product, so that scientist is also being supported in their vital work. Other people are contributing in significant, valuable ways so that the scientist can make a breakthrough and the product can be developed, put into production, marketed, distributed and improved. In fact, we would go so far as to say that however brilliant the scientist, if that support is not there at some level, then success will be highly elusive if not impossible.

Talent ecology and the truth about talent

A talented person is anyone that adds value to an enterprise or activity – a concept that is simultaneously simple, vital and often challenging.

The definition that 'talent' is the ability to generate value is significant. One of the most often debated points among people management professionals is how to determine 'potential' and 'talent', prompting the question 'potential for what'? How can you accurately predict someone's future capability to succeed in a leadership role? The key point is the emphasis on prediction, one that we believe is too loose and unreliable. It is time for a more tangible definition of talent: one that is more robust, reliable and dynamic than future predictions and guesswork given in an annual performance rating. A more rounded definition takes into account an individual's impact on their organization – the difference and value that result from their presence and their effort.

This definition (that 'talent' is the ability to generate value) gives us the truths about talent. One of the most significant truths is that talent requires the right environment in which to thrive. We call this *talent ecology* and it is the situation, culture and surroundings in which a firm's talent operates. Ecology is a great metaphor for talent; for example, it makes the point that talent does not exist in isolation but relies on its surroundings, it can be fragile, it grows and benefits from nurturing. This concept and its implications for leaders and organizations are discussed in detail later.

This definition of talent has several fundamental implications for leaders and their organizations. First, innovation, relationships and development are inextricably linked with talent. This means moving away from traditional approaches to managing people with a hierarchical focus on executive potential to an approach that favours those who can innovate, sell products or ideas, learn how to improve and do more and even change the way that the organization operates. These issues are at the heart of those organizations that are successful, and they are essential attributes of firms that can manage their talent. Working in this way may not make you the next CEO but it will bring vital knowledge, pivotal relationships and a practical 'can-do' approach that favours progress, ownership and personal responsibility. This is the type of talent our organizations will need and we need to think very differently about how best to attract and retain it.

This definition applies to not-for-profit organizations as well as commercial enterprises. For example, there can be little doubt that Gary Flandro's work as an intern made a major contribution to his organization, Nasa, and to the whole field of space exploration. Similarly, the *Washington Post* may be a commercial entity that has benefited hugely from the work of Woodward and Bernstein, but then so has the whole of their profession. They made journalism appear exciting, respected and cool – at least, for a while.

The second implication of this definition is that we now need to move beyond the idea that talent can be managed. Tangible assets can be managed but talented people and their potential cannot. You can only seduce, attract and inspire it. You can't manage talent. Think about it: *talent management* is an oxymoron. Trying to manage talent is like herding cats or nailing jello to a wall, without the wall. Why would you (and how could you) use *management*, a concept that historically comprizes planning, organizing, leading, directing, facilitating and controlling an organization, to control *talent*, with its own special ability or personal capacity for achievement? In fact, the notion of talent management was coined in the early 1990s by an IT software company marketing a new employee database. Talent management works with data; it doesn't work with people and their potential.

Another implication that springs from the definition of talent is the fact that it is *diverse* and much more ubiquitous than we might think. Sometimes it stands out but often it goes unnoticed and unfulfilled, linked to an individual's self-belief and an organization's capacity to engage with their employees. Those who confidently exhibit their strengths, are self-aware and take personal responsibility for their life and career, are more likely to find ways to add value, and this talent is more

Success is rarely an individual pursuit. Talent and value result from collaboration; this might be through team effort or through peer competition.

likely to be recognized. Equally, those who have yet to realize their capability require roles and environments that continually teach new skills and inspire self-belief. In each case, we believe that potential (meaning the ability to display talent and add value) is discretionary and that talent needs to be engaged rather than managed on its own terms. This concept of discretionary potential is also explored in detail later.

Given that talent is about adding value for an organization we should also think about building talented enterprises where our most capable people are focused on creating value and achieving their full potential, not simply chasing the next promotion and possibly over-reaching themselves. While value is generated by individuals, most often it is realized through teams and social networks inside and out of the organization. This means that we need to find people with diverse skills and experiences and value individuals and situations that are different to each other.

This approach is eloquently explained by HSBC, one of the world's largest financial services businesses. In their welcome pack for new employees joining their UK business they make this statement: 'In a world where a uniformity and standardisation dominate, we are building our business in the belief that different people from different cultures and different walks of life create value ... It is the combination of different people and the fusion of different ideas that provide the essential fuel for progress and success. At HSBC, diversity is something to be valued and celebrated. Working with colleagues from diverse backgrounds and cultures ensures greater understanding and insight. Diversity is not only an inescapable feature of our history and growth: it is the essence of our business. Our colleagues and our customers are of every culture, colour, belief, and ethnic group imaginable'.

Since businesses today need to create value in almost every area of their work this means adopting an abundant mindset to talent: it is no longer scarce, it is all around us. We just need to get better at creating environments that encourage it. This benefits every individual and their employer in a symbiotic relationship with the success of one relying on the success of the other. This mindset that talent is abundant also means revisiting the 'psychological contract' and understanding how work can be made more meaningful. It also requires that we look at the environment of our organizations: the concept of talent ecology.

Since businesses today need to create value in almost every area of their work this means adopting an abundant mindset to talent. It is no longer scarce, it is all around us. We just need to get better at finding it and engaging with it.

An individual's potential is both realized and, at times, constrained by the culture, interdependencies and leadership present in an organization. In this situation, we need to think less about the tall trees and much more about the whole forest. In management literature this is often referred to as a systemic approach, with the whole organization being more than the sum of its parts.

Generally speaking, talent, by which we mean the ability to create value, is abundant. The economic and social progress that has been enjoyed worldwide during the last 100 years has resulted from the efforts of the many, not the few. The recent years have seen this progress extend into whole new societies, including the BRIC and N11 countries mentioned earlier. Without doubt this 'progress' has caused severe problems as well, and what we have seen is a sporadic, unpredictable route to progress and greater productivity, punctuated by economic problems and business failure on a massive scale. We suspect that this haphazard progress reflects a haphazard and largely unsatisfactory way of managing people.

The truth about talent

Given that talent is abundant and defined by the way it creates value, talent management is much more about people and leadership and much less about anything else. One consequence of this view is that today's talent practices and attitudes are ageing and getting past their sell-by-date. In short, we believe that it is time to explode the idea of talent management. We have both worked in the area for many years, witnessing countless studies, surveys and projects. The conclusion to each of these is always the same; 'we don't have enough, quality people', 'we must do more', 'HR are not proficient', 'leaders are not giving this enough time' and so it goes. We wanted to get underneath the reason why we never have enough talent and why it appears to be so difficult to manage. We looked at practitioner case studies, prestigious academic articles and we talked with leaders in a number of commercial and non-profit organizations. We also conducted a unique, global study looking at people's beliefs about talent and how organizations deal with it. (This study compiled the views of almost 300 leading practitioners and executives worldwide.)

These studies suggested it was time to revisit first principles. We noticed that an entire industry had grown up around the idea of talent management including: software packages, consulting practices and special development programmes. Clearly, there are vested interests that have turned the process of 'talent management' into a specialized, mysterious black art. It need not be this way. Each of these is based on a shared belief that the talented are a small, exclusive group, 'the brightest and the best', that they should receive intensive investment, that their careers could be managed in a way that would enable them to succeed to the highest levels. And yet, more than a decade after the famous McKinsey study *War for Talent* research we could not find an organization that felt they had really succeeded in a way that met their needs.

HR leaders told us confidentially that when they invested in exclusive 'fast track' groups or talent pools they found it difficult to follow through with career moves; retention then became a major issue with those identified as 'talent'. Those in the talent groups talked to us of mismanaged expectations. Those outside the talent groups felt sidelined and disengaged. Despite these problems, leaders still questioned the quality of the supply and spent millions on external, executive recruitment.

One respondent commented: 'It's almost like you get one piece of the puzzle in the right place and the other pieces move around – it's like playing Tetris'. Another said: 'We have built a good fast track programme for our future leaders but it instils a sense of expectation of promotion we simply can't satisfy'.

It seems that conventional approaches to talent management have demanded substantial investment for little, if any, gain. Moreover, there is a growing unease that conventional approaches to talent management actually *destroy* the value in an organization.

What's more, despite seeing a whole industry emerge and human resources (HR) professionals mature and grow in sophistication, it didn't feel that we were closer to getting any better. Indeed, many of our participants in the global survey told us that the idea of talent management itself felt tainted and that the original goals of talent management felt even further away. In this respect talent management is a little like Soviet communism: an interesting, well-intentioned idea in theory but a disaster in practice, rooted in the previous century and now with a vast range of vested interests, and it is now outstaying its welcome.

This is when we realized that the fundamental beliefs around the whole area needed to be examined. These fundamental beliefs that we believe are flawed are:

Conventional approaches to talent management are a little like Soviet communism: an interesting, well-intentioned idea in theory but a disaster in practice, rooted in the previous century, now with a vast range of vested interests – and a concept that has definitely outstayed its welcome.

- There is not enough talent.
- Only the very brightest are talented.
- These people will become our future leaders.
- The lion's share of resource should be invested in them.
- HR's role is to accelerate the development of these individuals and engineer their careers.

We began to question how these assumptions stood up to the changes of the twenty-first century with its complex demographics, social fragmentation, globalization, emerging markets, technological progress, shifting expectations and priorities, economic boom and bust and new business models. We concluded that they are assumptions from a different time.

Our belief is that decades of investment in elite cadres of future executives have really not paid off. In this world talent was viewed as a scarce resource, there was never enough of it; potential was fixed and rare; those who were assessed as demonstrating the highest potential (usually those displaying similar characteristics to those who had already made it to the top) received dedicated investment, mentoring, intensive development, managed rotations and unsurprisingly they too made it to the top. The remaining 90% of the workforce received by comparison a disproportionate level of investment and, equally unsurprisingly, skills shortages in all areas widened. Now if the purpose of these Darwinian approaches to talent was to deliver succession plans and build more of the same then they were moderately successful. If the intention was to achieve anything else, then they have surely failed. We believe that the nature of business and work is changing so rapidly that investing solely in talent pools that take years to mature is static, complacent and commercially dangerous.

More than ever, talent operates systemically: talented people are attracted through relationships, developed through relationships and retained through relationships. The opposite also holds true.

We think it is time to think more carefully about the organizational context and to examine our assumptions about talent itself. We think that we are applying twentieth-century reductionist thinking to twenty-first-century challenges and people.

More than ever, talent operates systemically: talented people are attracted through relationships, developed through relationships and retained through relationships. The opposite also holds true.

Most challengingly, we believe that everyone in the organization has a role to play in strengthening the supply of talent. This is not just about how we help people build their skills and capabilities and achieve their potential, it is also about how we structure the nature of work itself. Crucially it is the *talent ecology* of an organization that determines success: by which we mean how the organization functions, why it exists, what it values and how it changes. We need to concentrate on the organizational context for talent, looking more closely at the forest of tall trees. Because, when it comes to the talent debate, we quite literally have not been able to see the wood for the trees.

On this basis there are several truths about talent that need to be considered and discussed.

We are all talent now

Organizations must think about their talent ecology: how they can build a culture where everyone has a role to play in making the organization successful. Imagine the power of realizing the potential of an entire workforce, not just the stellar careers of a chosen few.

Talent is abundant and diverse

For organizations and people to succeed, managers need to believe in the talents and potential of all their people. The alternative, continuing to behave in a way that suggests it is rare, will alienate many people in current and future generations and produce behaviour in future leaders that is short-term and self serving.

The talented are those who generate value, not merely those who can get to the top

This success might be achieved by reinventing products, market relationships and the model of the business itself.

Potential is discretionary

This idea has two elements. First, employees' effort, commitment and engagement are all on loan to their employer, and second, people can often accomplish much more than they or anyone else might think. As a result, organizations need to find better ways to attract, inspire and particularly *engage* their people. Just as the difference between elite athletes is often very close, so the difference between great firms that are competing is also very fine – the difference is often the degree to which employees excel. Leaders need to help their people achieve their potential and excel; that makes work more satisfying for everyone than simply doing the minimum.

Growing and engaging talent is at the core of leadership

This links closely with the previous point and being able to engage talent requires great insight and skill. This is surely one of the most significant managerial capabilities. If you doubt it, consider this: how many of the world's greatest businesses are ghastly employers? The relationship between working and employment practices and business success is certainly complex but experience suggests that there is undeniably a correlation.

HR must reinvent itself to deliver practices for a 'workforce of one'

Work must become more meaningful for employees and meaning is highly individual. To achieve this, employee propositions must be highly customized and flexible.

Talented people are attracted to talented places

Leaders need to pay greater attention to the way the organization works; talented teams, networks, experimentation, openness and flexibility all matter a great deal. Ignore them and the talented ignore you.

So, how many Gary Flandros are sitting quietly in the corner of your workplace? Do they feel able to make a real, lasting contribution to your organization? The truth about talent is that they could, if only we took a different, better approach and displayed leadership that reflects the times in which we live.

In this book we focus on several vital questions for leaders and their organizations. For example, why, despite their good intentions, are leaders unable to find, manage and develop the talented people they need? How do you attract good people to your organization and how can you ensure that they achieve their full potential? How do you stimulate, engage and inspire people at all levels to achieve greatness? How is the workplace changing and are there new rules for employment in the twenty-first century? What practical support do people really want at work and what do they get? Above all, how can you build a dynamic workforce, help people realize their potential and enable them to succeed?

These questions and, indeed, this whole book, highlight a particularly significant and possibly controversial issue. This is the view that we all have talents. We can all find things that we will fail at, and we can all be ordinary or average at many, many things, but also we all have gifts and talents. It is surely up to each of us, supported by our leaders and our employers, to find these talents and achieve as much as we possibly can with them. This is not only the progressive, competitive and self-interested thing to do, it also happens to be the right thing to do. That is the truth about talent.

In the next chapter we look at current views of talent and consider why, increasingly, they are outdated and inadequate. We explain how our understanding of talent needs to be reviewed and why we need to adopt a more inclusive approach. As an alternative we highlight the notion of *discretionary potential* – one of the fundamental truths about talent and a new way of thinking about this vital issue.

Chapter 2

A New Way of Thinking About Talent

How organizations think about talent

What is talent – would you know it if you saw it? More importantly, how is it relevant to your organization? These questions are fundamental to the talent debate and yet we often stall at the first one: what is talent? In business as in life talent has become defined as 'those with a special gift or ability'. 'Special' denotes unusual or rare, conjuring images of incredible prodigies such as Mozart or athletes such as Usain Bolt. In recent years talent has become closely associated with stardom; from American Idol's Kelly Clarkson to Susan Boyle in Britain's Got Talent, it's a well-worn story about an individual battling personal hardship and breaking out of anonymity to achieve celebrity status.

These associations play out into the way we think about talent in organizations. We have superstar CEOs and international investment bankers who attract the title 'masters of the Universe'. This view has been supported in recent years by HR practices dedicated to spotting and nurturing high potential 'executive talent'. This has created elite *talent pools*: people who receive dedicated attention, investment and reward throughout their careers. These individuals are indeed talented and influential; however, we believe this 'narrow, rare and special' way of thinking about talent has become dated.

Why? Very simply: because this view of talent will not grow or sustain organizations in the future.

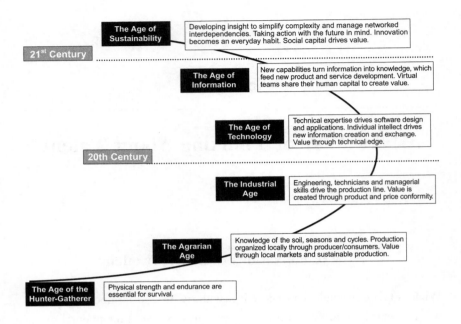

The Age of Sustainability — Developing insight to simplify complexity and manage networked interdependencies. Taking action with the future in mind. Innovation becomes an everyday habit. Social capital drives value.

21st Century

The Age of Information — New capabilities turn information into knowledge, which feed new product and service development. Virtual teams share their human capital to create value.

The Age of Technology — Technical expertise drives software design and applications. Individual intellect drives new information creation and exchange. Value through technical edge.

20th Century

The Industrial Age — Engineering, technicians and managerial skills drive the production line. Value is created through product and price conformity.

The Agrarian Age — Knowledge of the soil, seasons and cycles. Production organized locally through producer/consumers. Value through local markets and sustainable production.

The Age of the Hunter-Gatherer — Physical strength and endurance are essential for survival.

What we mean by talent

It could even be argued that this approach to talent identification and promotion has played a role in creating a generation of executives who believe themselves to be invincible. The problem is not that they are not talented (because many are bright, driven and dedicated individuals) but the organization's over-reliance on one, particular type of talent – one based on managerial competence, that is the ability to perform at increasingly more senior levels. We are also sceptical about how talent has become synonymous with 'high potential', believing that basing a whole talent strategy only on those few who might succeed at the very top levels tomorrow is, at best, expensive crystal ball gazing.

There is also a growing frustration among executives about the return on investment from today's talent management practices. Without exception, everyone wants more capable people and yet few believe that the actions they are taking will actually achieve this result. In conversation with our survey participants we found that many share this disappointment and offer detailed insight into why this is the case and how it can be resolved. Their responses point to a view of talent that is more grounded and tangible:

one which is based on contribution today, rather than potential tomorrow. In fact, three important points stand out in these responses:

- That the talented are those who change things.
- That we need to get better at harnessing the latent talents of employees across the whole organization.
- That this definition of talent transcends national boundaries and is equally cited across Europe, the US, South America, Middle East and Asia.

When you get down to the details, however, important adaptations with local cultures do take place. These relate to how the leaders who are changing things actually operate, the nature of their results, and how this contributes to the broader organization. This underlines the point that context is vitally important, as well as the need to ensure that talent activity is linked with the business's ambition and strategy as well as the economic environment. Ultimately it is this, and not an individual's ability, that drives how talent is valued. As one executive commented:

The way that senior executives in organizations think about talent is increasingly outdated, ineffective and self-sustaining. It focuses on selecting a few brilliant individuals who will lead the organization in the future – they receive all the opportunities and resources and, unsurprisingly, make it to the top. What about the talent and potential in everyone else? What about the unpredictability of the future? This view of talent will not grow or sustain organizations in the future.

'Talent' is driven by the context and needs of the organization: the skills and qualities needed by one business at one point in time could be completely different to those needed in a different sector at a different point in the economic cycle.

Another executive reflected that:

A superb speech writer is overlooked when the company needs the speaker.

Talent is a dynamic concept – one that changes in value according to an organization's economic circumstances. Our respondents also believe as we do that if successful organizations are operating in increasingly complex, competitive environments – then they will need a more diverse range of talents to succeed. The range of talents required will be determined by the business strategy and will vary by sector and market conditions. The smart companies will look for talent in new or unusual places. This means looking beyond the executive potential track and towards the 'vital core' and the front-line.

Our research also suggests that organizations require a new definition of talent, one that capitalizes on the potential of the *whole* workforce. We have seen very little return on the persistent focus on 'high potentials' and believe it is time to make talent more tangible. Our research suggests that now and in the future talent is about those who can generate sustainable value, not those who can get to the top. This might be by developing products, market relationships and the business itself. These are the people who can build critical relationships, people who can provide insight from data and people who can create new products and services. These are the new leaders of the organization and finding them isn't about their potential to move up into increasingly senior positions. It's about how they perform now and how they deliver tangible and sustainable results.

Talent is about those who can generate sustainable value, not those who can get to the top. The range of talents required will be determined by the business strategy and will vary by sector and market conditions. The smart companies will look for talent in new or unusual places. This means looking beyond the executive potential track and towards the 'vital core' and the front-line.

How talent management is changing

Turn around. Look around. What do you see? Markets rule but protestors are marching against global capitalism. The NASDAQ composite index has gone down the drain. Disasters have cast their daunting shadows. Perils are lurking at every corporate corner. Teargas has hung in the air of Seattle, Gothenburg and Genoa. Stock markets have evaporated. Docu-soaps have invaded our living rooms. Corporations like ABB and Enron have been turned upside down and inside out. In brief: bricks and bullets, bubbles, bin Laden, big brother, and bosses bad to the bone.

Preface to *Karaoke Capitalism* by Jonas Ridderstrale and
Kjell Nordstrom.

As we enter the second decade of the twenty-first century it is striking to see that our patterns of trade and organization are much changed, even from those in play at the start of the new millennium. Economically, power is shifting from West to East. Against this backdrop, consumers are becoming more choosy and more active. We are also consuming differently, at times of our choosing and in many different ways. More than ever, our choices are influenced by what we believe and how we want to present ourselves to the world. Our individual place in society (what a marketer would call a demographic niche) and our own relative wealth further complicate these choices. Each personal 'twist' generates huge complexity for those delivering their services to us. Could we have imagined the economic and social shifts that have taken place in less than a decade? We explain the implications for twenty-first century leaders in Chapter 9; here, we detail three of the most significant forces shaping a new approach to the way talent is

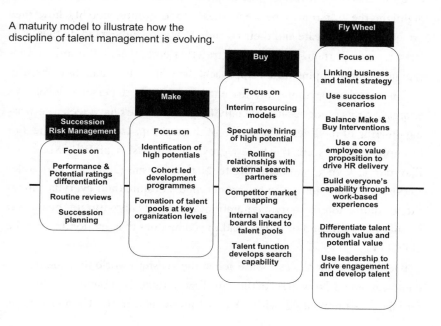

A maturity model to illustrate how the discipline of talent management is evolving.

Succession Risk Management
Focus on
Performance & Potential ratings differentiation
Routine reviews
Succession planning

Make
Focus on
Identification of high potentials
Cohort led development programmes
Formation of talent pools at key organization levels

Buy
Focus on
Interim resourcing models
Speculative hiring of high potential
Rolling relationships with external search partners
Competitor market mapping
Internal vacancy boards linked to talent pools
Talent function develops search capability

Fly Wheel
Focus on
Linking business and talent strategy
Use succession scenarios
Balance Make & Buy Interventions
Use a core employee value proposition to drive HR delivery
Build everyone's capability through work-based experiences
Differentiate talent through value and potential value
Use leadership to drive engagement and develop talent

viewed and managed. These relate to the supply of labour, the availability
of the right skills, and consumption.

A fragmented, fluctuating supply of labour

Demographic predictions on age and birth rates are playing out all around
us, resulting in many new and unexpected trends. Despite the aging workforce the rate of retirement has not increased as dramatically as people
anticipated. People continue to stay in work
beyond 60 and with changing state retirement
ages this is likely to increase. Economics are
the single biggest reason for this, with stock
market values fluctuating and as billions are
wiped off pension values this is likely to
continue.

*Talent is not about someone's
potential to move into
increasingly senior positions. It's
about how they perform now and
how they deliver tangible and
sustainable results.*

These 'Baby Boomers' (born 1943–60) are now joined in the workforce
by their 'Generation X' (1961–81) and 'Generation Y/Millennials' (1982–
2000) counterparts. The significance of these groups is their numbers and
their expectations of work. Boomers are in the largest supply and still dominate the executive level of most major corporations. Many commentators
highlight the differences between these three groups, notably how they
prefer to communicate and their attitude to work. Understanding these differences is important, although one trap that employers fall into is stereo-
typing. A more sophisticated approach is to find out what they share in
common and understand how to engage them on a personal level. We
emphasize this point because socially the last ten years have seen a surprising blurring of the lines in how each of these groups live and consume. For
example, Boomers are the fastest growing purchasers of WII, Xbox and
Playstation. 'Gen Y' and their 'Digital Native' cousins (2000–to date) prefer
face-to-face communication over other media despite their everyday appetite for online interactivity. Generation X-ers typically saturate the market
for all new media and of course lead the companies that are dominating the
digital era.

Back in 2000, there was a sense across the Western world that unemployment was tamed. Now in six of the world's wealthiest economies, the demand
for labour is unravelling, with 10% unemployment in the US and France,

almost 8% in the UK, Italy and Germany and a shocking 19% in Spain (as at December 2009). Unemployment has also grown across the BRIC countries (Brazil, Russia, India and China), however the relative strength of these economies has meant that their labour markets appear more buoyant.

The recession of 2008–10 has meant that low value work continues to follow the lowest unit of cost and move overseas. New players in West Africa and Eastern Europe emerge to take on this work while India moves up the value chain, offering outsourced support in areas as broad as software design, pharmaceutical research and development and retail financial services. This global demand for outsourcing will continue to grow as firms reorganize their operating structures in an effort to save money. This outsourced work is now taking place through numerous alliances and partnerships. Against this backdrop, it is hard to agree with the prediction that 'there is not enough talent', particularly when the generally optimistic 'Millennials' face the highest rate of graduate unemployment in a generation.

From the credit crunch to the capability crunch

Despite this over-supply of labour a perceived lack of talent continues to keep many CEOs awake at night. Our discussions with executives tell us that this anxiety is not simply about not having enough supply: it's about not having the right mix of capabilities. These are the skills needed to be competitive, to innovate and to build a sustainable business. The problem

We in the West are failing employers with an insufficient and irrelevant mix of skills, but we are also failing our children just at a time when we need them to be the most versatile and resilient generation in history.

is the speed at which these capabilities are needed and rate at which they change.

Consider the curriculum in universities today. The research, validation, design, teaching and assessment timeline can take several years to complete. This means that it is not unusual for the class of 2010 to have been taught cases from the turn of the century. We are teaching our children skills for a different age, a situation that has been described by UNICEF's Global Head of Education as 'static knowledge'. So, despite the unprecedented numbers of people achieving degrees and A grades, this historical time lag plays out across the education system. This situation also combines with worrying increases in social exclusion, with many young people falling behind and opting out.

These problems are evident not just in *what* we teach but also *how* we teach. Our schools and colleges are already struggling with a generational learning gap; how today's digital natives make sense of the cold formality of the classrooms and lecture halls. Martin Bean, the newly appointed Vice Chancellor of the UK's Open University cautioned the education community to be alert to a 'crisis of relevance'. This was a reference to the educational subject matter and also to the educators themselves.

The fundamental problem with our education systems is that they were invented in the nineteenth century to provide a workforce for an industrial age. Despite being created over a century ago many of the beliefs and practices remain. There is the teacher as expert at the front of the class, the age-based cohorts, the line-ups and bells – it's still reminiscent of a 1950's movie.

The tragedy here is that we are not living in a golden age: we are living in a world where humanity is facing some of its biggest challenges. We in the West are failing employers with an insufficient and irrelevant skills mix, but we are also failing our children just at a time when we need them to be the most versatile and resilient generation in history. The case for a fundamental change in education is made in the compelling film '*We Are the People We've Been Waiting For*' (released in November 2009). The film has been called 'An Inconvenient Truth for Education' and opens with the quote from HG Wells: 'The future is a race between education and catastrophe'. We think this is a vital contribution to the talent debate.

Connected consumption

The following random facts demonstrate our growing appetite for a new type of communication.

- In December 2008, 110.4 billion text messages were sent in the USA, rising from 2.1 billion just five years earlier.
- In only seven years from its inception in 2003, Skype now has the largest share of the world's long distance phone market with over 500 million users.
- 44% of baby boomers in the US own a Playstation, WII or XBOX.

- Facebook is the third most popular website for seniors. It has a population the size of the USA.
- 71% of US children (12–17 years) own a mobile phone.
- After the USA, Brazil is the second biggest Twitter user, Turkey is the second biggest Facebook user, China has the biggest mobile phone market.
- The *New York Times* is read by almost 2 million readers on Twitter.
- 80% of European 'Tweenies' (8–14 years) have internet access. 74% use this for games and 59% for homework. Face-to-face communication is their most preferred medium.
- The average salary of the LinkedIn user is $110,000 – far higher than users on other social networks.
- There are nearly 20 million bloggers in the US and 450,000 of these earn their living from blogging.
- The average time a US adult spends on-line has doubled since 1999 to 13 hours a week.
- Almost a third of the UK's population now subscribe to on-line, personalized radio.

It is tempting to reflect on these fast-changing facts and say 'so what?' The point is that the skills required and available for work are changing, and so is the character and expectations of the workforce. There may not be a clash of generations but there is a need to understand the different skills, experiences, expectations and aspirations of an increasingly broad workforce. Despite these changes, in the workplace it seems that understanding of the diversity of the workforce is often limited, technology is fast but still not wholly integrated, and gaps in pay and expectations between employees and directors seem likely to increase.

Where we are today: the problem with current views of 'talent' in organizations

Look at talent management practices in most major companies today and we guarantee that they will be built on at least one of the following elements:

- A long range approach to succession planning.
- A drive to identify 'high potential' individuals able to move into those plans.
- A focus on generalist skills or executive potential.

These practices share several fundamental assumptions from a different business age. These lock talent management into a forecasting mindset, and while popular and effective in the 1970s, they lack the dynamism to cope with the uncertainty of today's market conditions.

The belief that the future can be managed: from succession to scenario planning

Succession planning is an exercise in managing risk. Done well, it provides a visible snapshot of the *current* supply of capable individuals who could succeed in key roles. This is important when you need to check coverage of key positions and when recruitment decisions are required for an imminent departure. It is much more difficult, however, to tie this *current* supply to the *future* demand picture. Establishing demand relies on being able to anticipate the future operating environment. Will we be growing or consolidating the balance sheet? Will we be market leading or building market share? Will we be acquiring or divesting? Will our operating model be different? Where will we be located? And so on. Each of these major questions requires different types of skills and qualities.

The connection between strategy and talent management is explored in detail in Chapter 4, and strategy plays a crucial role in the way that talent is – and should be – managed. However, in our experience few organizations work this through in a practical way that connects strategy with talent. In most cases this subtlety is often overlooked and the benchmark is set against the existing operating environment, or the qualities of the person who does the role now, or both. Today's benchmark becomes the lens through which future successors are identified and developed. At each succession review the pipeline is honed, weeding out those who have had a bad year, an unsuccessful project or a run in with the CEO. New joiners must wait until the next review. And it is rare that people are added back in once they have been taken out. We have heard this justified by a need to be 'more robust', to 'improve calibration' but it just makes the talent pool smaller and less diverse. This in turn limits the available choice for future successors and the organization's ability to respond to changes in the future. Organizationally, we believe this thinning out of the pool limits the business's ability to respond to changing circumstances. In this sense, despite the arguments of robustness, a smaller talent pool is a weaker pool, especially where there are similar skills and capabilities. Commercially, this approach to succession planning means firms are basing a sizeable investment on a small population who are untested and are in many cases relatively unknown.

In the excellent book *Talent on Demand* (Harvard Business Publishing, 2008) Peter Cappelli suggests that we can manage unpredictability by applying supply chain management and scenario planning techniques. He shares the challenges of Capital One, whose workforce first halved then doubled across a seven-year period. An expert group of marketing and operations research specialists was brought together to work on a more dynamic means of modelling the workforce. This group integrated the available people and business data then applied sophisticated data mining techniques. Customized talent planning scenarios were then provided for each business unit.

> Rather than just predict the number of people required in each role, they also modeled outcomes such as attrition rates, employee morale, rates of promotion and outside hires. Rather than generating a static estimate of how many workers will be needed two years out they say to operating managers: 'Tell us the assumptions you have about your business, and we'll give you a talent estimate. Better yet, give us a range of different assumptions, and we'll give you a range of talent estimates within which the reality will most likely lie'.
>
> Peter Cappelli, *Talent on Demand*

The business conditions for talent are a critical part of the organization's talent ecology. Notice also, the breadth of data used to inform the analysis of likely demand: this marries business estimates with employee trends. Thinking in terms of how the business's situation and plans play out in a range of scenarios is a good way of getting to grips with the capabilities required for the future.

This far-sighted, scenario-based approach is also influencing the work of executive search firms, particularly in the work of CEO succession. Here the project is less about finding the ideal candidate and more about generating a candidate pool with the capacity to meet a range of market circumstances. Stephen Langton from search firm Heidrich & Struggles comments on how their work is evolving in a project with Qantas:

> Halfway through that succession the economy collapsed, it went from being one of the world's fastest-growing airlines to a 'Mayday' situation. One must have the courage to see this process as an evolving thing, not a transaction where all terms are set up front. When priorities change, the right individual for the role may start to look somewhat different. Boards are beginning to see this as a rolling process. For our main succession clients we're reassessing the top team every six months. In the future, this process won't be an isolated event; it will be like an accountancy firm looking after your finances. The relationship will be ongoing.
>
> *Reproduced by permission of Stephen Langton, Heidrich & Struggles and Global Trade Media*

The belief that we can spot our future leaders today (and manage their careers)

A dilemma that organizations now grapple with is how to balance external recruitment with internal development of the pipeline of leaders. This is more sophisticated than simply deciding on how many to recruit or promote in each instance – it's a question of attracting some and retaining others. In both cases, the organization needs real clarity on *what and who* they are looking for. For many, a way of resolving this issue has been through recruiting and developing those with 'high potential' – those with the ability to progress to more senior roles comparatively more quickly than their counterparts. The danger in this approach is that you build a pipeline of future leaders based on past needs.

The march of the 'high potentials'

The belief that future leaders can be hired and developed today has become the bedrock of popular talent practices. It plays well with senior executives, many of whom were groomed through similar approaches. Graduate recruitment rounds, MBA programmes, speculative hiring, assessment centres, internal high flyer programmes all stem from this belief. These practices in and of themselves are benign and modestly effective.

Increasingly however, these long-range, cohort-centred development activities get in the way of real talent development in several ways:

- The learning outcomes rarely tie into business strategy – this may mean we are developing capabilities for an imagined (rather than actual) future.
- It is difficult to tie up programme alumni with openings, making it difficult to deploy individuals to roles when they are needed.
- As individuals recognize their value and move elsewhere attrition rates rise and retention of key skills becomes harder.
- Employees not on these programmes have a haphazard and modest development experience. This can lead to disengagement and deterioration of skills across the wider workforce.

This is an issue not just of lead times and logistics but also of what is valued by the organization, how this is identified and rewarded. Increasingly 'talent' has become synonymous with 'high potential'.

A generic definition of 'high potential' is someone who is demonstrating an ability to perform effectively at the next level. The relative rate of progress ('promotability') is also important in these definitions. Those identified as being able to progress faster than their peers, usually a grade every two years, fall into this category.

Psychologists tell us that these individuals stand out by their superior intellect, social skills and personal drive. These assessments are benchmarked against a *historically successful executive population* and a relative rating is awarded. Two things stand out here which are in conflict with the task of assessing future potential. Firstly, that we are benchmarking backwards (not forwards), and secondly that the benchmark is already successful. It's interesting to note that we have worked in several organizations where this psychological assessment has been validated against actual progression of those rated as high potential, and there is very little correlation.

More surprising is that when the 'high potentials' are reviewed against the progress of those not rated as having potential, the rate of progress is the same!

Potential for what?

This is not to demolish a whole of school of psychological theory in a paragraph (psychological assessments provide valuable insights into personal abilities and drivers), but rather to explain the importance of how the organization really works and the assumptions on which it relies. For organizations, today's answer to the *potential for what?* question is all about moving up a level. These levels are often operational. For example, moving from manager to senior manager or Business Unit MD, and then on to Chief Executive. In their excellent book *The Leadership Pipeline* Ram Charan, Stephen Drotter and James Noel bring the scale of these levels to life. They describe the capabilities required at six 'leadership passages' running up through the organization.

The first passage is about managing yourself and performing effectively. The second is the first step into managing others and taking line responsibility for front-line teams. The third passage is the functional leader who reports to multifunction general managers. At this level, functional managers, need to become skilled at taking other functional concerns and needs into consideration. The fourth passage, to business manager, requires a major shift in capability and focus. The manager is becoming more oriented to strategic rather than operational goals. The fifth passage, to group manager, requires four critical skill sets: evaluating strategy for capital allocation and deployment, developing business managers, leading the portfolio strategy and assessing core capabilities. The sixth passage, to enterprize manager, focuses more on *value* than skills. The leader must be a long-term, visionary thinker.

In one example, an executive promoted up two levels, from functional to group level, retained his functional thinking and values and failed as a result. The authors comment that while his grade may have changed, his way of looking at the world had not: 'He was operating out of a purely functional value system: Can we do it? This is different from the value system of a business manager: Should we do it? And it's quite different from the value system of a group executive: Which choice will give us the best result now and in the future?'

We believe that effective organizations require all employees to exercise a degree of CEO-type wisdom, values and initiative. We also think that the levels discussed by Charan, Drotter and Noel will converge. This will be driven by cost (and further re-structuring) but also by the need for speed and relationships. Six levels like the ones described introduce too much complexity into the system and mean that decisions are taken further away from where the action is.

The action we are referring to is not managerial action but real interaction at the edges of the organization, with customers, with communities and with ideas.

The action we are referring to is not managerial action but real interaction at the edges of the organization, with customers, with communities and with ideas.

The leadership pipeline is a simple and effective way of thinking about the critical question: 'potential for what?' Even so, it is important that we challenge the assumption that only the most senior leaders are visionary, only they get to exercise an enterprize-wide mindset and value system. We also need to look critically at the other underlying assumption of the 'career ladder': implying that people are willing to stay with the organization long enough to clamber up through these levels.

Being insightful

Vision and the passion to progress are vitally important characteristics of talent. They are the qualities people follow in leaders. Sixty-three per cent of our survey participants identified them as two of the top three indicators of talent. This is a subtle shift from conventional thinking on judgement, drive and influence being the most important indicators of talent.

When we asked survey respondents what they thought were the most important characteristics of talent we found they favoured the following attributes:

1. Insight – 68%
2. Passion – 63%
3. Vision – 63%
4. Judgement – 58.5%
5. Drive – 56%
6. Influence – 49%

All of these of course are related. Topping the poll, however, is a surprise: 'Insight'. The ability to find opportunities or create meaning from complexity is viewed as the most important quality for talent today. The dictionary definition of insight is revealing.

1. The capacity to discern the true nature of a situation; penetration.
2. The act or outcome of grasping the inward or hidden nature of things or of perceiving in an intuitive manner.
3. Deep, thorough, or mature understanding.

Almost 70% of our survey participants believe that intuition, discernment and deep understanding are the qualities that signal talent today. When we probed these responses we learned that the ability to be insightful is essential for working through the complexity of today's workplace. One of our participants summarized why this is so important:

> Getting things done is no longer a matter of moving A to B. You have to take the temperature of a place, read between the lines on what's really important. If you can't do this you'll be overwhelmed and fail.

On a more optimistic note, another described their perception of insight as:

> Being able to see the potential in a situation and understanding how to play this.

In this sense, being insightful is essential to performing well at work. It represents a shift away from simply doing things right, towards doing the right thing. It is about acting wisely, being able to discern the issues of *what* and *why* in a situation, rather than just *how*. This reflects the growing mood for a new style of leadership; one that is thoughtful and accountable. It is telling that talent is becoming synonymous with leadership but not in a hierarchical sense. Our participants talked consistently of talent being widely available and untapped at every level of the organization, commenting that:

> Being talent is not a badge from HR or a grade, it's about how you are and how you change things.

Here we are reminded of the French name for change agents, 'Animateurs', a term used by writer Peter Senge in his book *The Necessary Revolution* (page 147). The Animateur is the person who quite literally brings things to life, providing a new way of seeing or interacting that creates focus and energy. Senge draws the connection back to leadership and the importance of being inspirational, reminding us that the verb 'to inspire' comes from the Latin 'inspiraie', meaning quite literally 'to breathe life into'. Talent is perhaps more of a verb than an adjective. It is less a description of an individual and more a way of describing how people work and the contribution they make.

Moving beyond the usual suspects ...

Many of our research participants talked about the need to value insight, passion and vision in the front-line, with technical specialists and also with the groups known as 'B-players'. In all cases, however, there was an acknowledgement that the level of experience determined the scale of difference an individual could make. There was a strong view that experience was the most important way of generating these qualities. The organizational environment they were operating in was also important, with many commenting on the pivotal role of the line manager – a relationship that could make or break how an individual's potential was realized in the organization.

Talent is perhaps more of a verb than an adjective. It is less a description of an individual and more a way of describing how people work and the contribution they make.

The importance of looking for talent in these alternative groups is gaining in popularity. McKinsey's 2009 article on *Unlocking the Potential of Front-line Managers* talked about how decision-making power needed to relocate back to the shop floor. Their cases show how customer demand requires immediate and outstanding service. This means freeing service staff to make decisions on the ground, and the need to look for opportunities to edge out the competition. It doesn't mean waiting for a policy statement or a 'how-to guide' from Head Office. The front-line is, after all, where customers are won and lost. It is also the part of the organization that experiences the highest level of employee turnover in almost every industry. We have to rethink our assumptions that people operating at this level always require less sophisticated skills than their senior executive counterparts. The front-line manager's talent for balancing their work priorities and coaching their teams to do the same is becoming increasingly important.

An interesting perspective on this issue is provided by Time Warner. This corporation views all its employees as potential talent and employs a 'Leaders Teaching Leaders' approach across the business. This is not a top down approach: it's an effective means of sharing practice and company values. Time Warner's Chief Learning Officer, Pat Crull, describes this in the following way (CEO.com December 2009):

> It's a way of keeping a finger on the pulse of our organization. Learning is a two-way process. Employees learn from their leaders, and executives learn a great deal from interacting with customer-facing employees, who report back on their first-hand experience of what customers want. Executive education is clearly a priority, as well as focusing on developing customer-facing employees within the organization, whether they are our installers, our techs visiting customers' homes, or agents in our call centres, we have so much focus on customer services. We know these are our heroes.
>
> *Reproduced by permission of globaltrademedia.com*

This wider, more inclusive approach emphasizes the importance of technical players. The renewable energy industry is still developing and Danish company Vestas offers a comprehensive framework for different types of talent across its 20,000 strong workforce. Vestas' purpose is:

> To stay competitive and consolidate our position as No. 1 in modern energy. We are convinced that the programmes for specialists, project managers and managers will bring us closer to our employees' personal and professional development – and have a positive effect on the bottom line.

With many employees, work is less about reaching a career goal or ceiling and more about making a conscious choice about the content, purpose, fulfilment and reward of their work.

The skills that Vestas requires are in short supply in an emerging industry and it makes sense to focus on the areas required for growth. Here is a talent strategy shaped to the purpose of the business. This shift towards including technicians is also being generated by a diminishing supply of specialists in the labour market. Specialists operate on a different career pattern to generalist 'high potentials'. Their education is lengthier and their opportunity to move between sectors is wider. The resulting demand has given rise to reward hotspots. This was first noticeable with IT professionals and the much anticipated millennium bug, and we are seeing it again with risk professionals in the financial services sector. In all cases, talent is defined by what the specialist can deliver now and, sometimes, the opportunity cost or issues encountered by not having them.

The rise of discretionary potential

The concern about mitigating the loss of talent is one of the factors influencing the revival of another alternative group, the 'B Players'. First popularized by Thomas J DeLong, the term refers to those who form the 'heart and soul' of the organization. They are distinguished from the 'A Players', the organization's stars (an alternative term for executive high potentials or the top 15% of performers) in that they are deemed to have achieved their career ceiling. And, unlike their 'C Player' counterparts (the bottom 15% of underperformers) the 'B Players' create the 'ballast of the organization' by performing consistently and effectively. While DeLong's categorization of the workforce has been criticized as over simplistic and condescending, it does underline a critical point in the talent debate: do not underestimate or disengage segments of your workforce, they exercise discretionary potential.

We prefer to think of the 'B Players' as a segment because when you get to know them you begin to appreciate that sitting in this group is less about reaching a career ceiling and more about making a conscious choice about their own work. Sometimes this choice relates to making more time for family commitments, sometimes it's about developing mastery in a specialist area, sometimes it's about opting out of the corporate career game. We believe that the decision to opt out of the 'A Player' stream is more prevalent than we realize. Conventional wisdom holds that people's careers stop when their performance drops or when they reach the limit of their capability. We believe it's much more subtle and personally driven. It's about what's important to the individual and whether this connects with what's important to the organization at a given time. In this sense, an individual's potential is theirs to share and they are likely only to do this with the people, projects and places they believe in.

People forming part of this group hold invaluable experience. Theirs is a latent talent that has been curiously overlooked. Engaging the individuals in this group is vitally important. Organizations will need to employ a mass customization approach since the size of the group is large and their requirements are individual.

A more tangible view of talent

We prefer to think about potential as an individual's capacity for generating value, rather than being effective at the next level. Crucially, the ability to generate value is demonstrated through tangible outcomes. Our survey participants described this as being visibly outstanding, being able to effect change in the company environment, its services, its customers or its people.

This emphasis on keeping talent real and practical is evident throughout the responses to our research and our discussions with executives. Being able to consistently deliver results that have a '*differential impact*' is a consistent theme. And, the way these results are delivered is also important. The talented people are those who are able to create the conditions for others to succeed. These are not lone wolves, they are social operators, able to tune into the requirements of an environment and work through to the result.

Our survey gave participants a range of ten widely-used descriptions of talent and asked them to highlight a definition. The following definitions made it to the top five:

1. A high performer
2. A leader
3. Standing out from the crowd
4. An innovator
5. An inspirational teacher

When you think of someone who is talented, what characteristics do they display? (Participants rated the following items on a scale from 1 to 5, where 1 is the least influential and 5 the most.)

Likely characteristics of talented executives

	1	2	3	4	5	N/A
Intelligence	1%	2%	7%	45%	45%	(N/A)
Insight	0%	0%	5%	26%	68%	1%
Judgement	0%	2%	6%	31%	58%	3%
Influence	1%	0%	16%	33%	49%	1%
Flair	2%	8%	28%	32%	27%	3%
Drive	0%	3%	11%	27%	56%	3%
Creativity	0%	3%	13%	44%	37%	3%
Passion	0%	0%	5%	27%	64%	4%
Vision	0%	0%	6%	26%	64%	4%
Sociability	1%	8%	26%	46%	19%	0%

We also gave participants the opportunity to create their own definition of talent. There was a surprising degree of agreement about the need to 'make a contribution' and 'leave a legacy' 'whatever the role or the skill'. The importance of 'edge' was also repeated. Participants describe people as demonstrating edge in a variety of ways, from 'achieving mastery' in a particular discipline through to being able to 'make change happen'. The descriptions create a picture of people who are able to move things forward by applying themselves. They also point to a character that is agile and self-conscious. This self-consciousness is applied to their own learning, they seek out and act on feedback and they also use it to tune into the needs of the people they work with. This focus on others is heavily underlined. Many participants comment on the 'talent anti-hero', that is the individual who displays many of the characteristics described but, and this is a crucial distinction, acts selfishly. As one participant commented:

No matter how brilliant, people are not talent when achieving their personal ambition is their over-riding goal. They have to contribute to the wider purpose.

The importance of integrity is cited by many as the essential component of the character of talent. These are individuals who weigh up the difference they aim to make – today and in the future. Theirs is a sustainable style of leadership, one that takes action conscious of the impact they make on others and the wider organization.

How do you make a difference?

This is a more tangible definition of talent, one that asks people to reflect on: what is different as a result of you? How have you made a difference? There is little science required for this – it is simply a matter of looking at an individual's results and judging how these results contribute value to the company. This requires a clear explanation of value and what this looks like for every individual in the organization. This will, of course, differ in scale according to role and experience but practically we should set objectives and review evidence in the following areas:

- What have you improved or invented which takes our business forward?
- How have you used the resources you control responsibly?
- How have you contributed to the results of other colleagues?
- How have you strengthened our relationship with our customers and the wider community?

Put simply, it's a question of face outward and focus on innovation. This is as relevant for call centre workers as it is for public servants. We also don't accept the notion that innovation is out of reach for junior or front-line colleagues, they are often best placed to find, generate or seize opportunities. The crucial point is how an individual can realize an opportunity and this is the most important indicator of talent.

Leadership reflections

- Do you understand how employees create value in your organization?
- How is the creation of value communicated and rewarded in your organization?
- Is your performance system still focused on activity and tasks rather than outcomes and results?

- In what ways do you help people make the connection between the work that they do and how your business impacts on the wider community?
- How do you see talent in your workforce? Do you adopt an inclusive whole workforce view, or an exclusive 'high potential' perspective? Have you reviewed the business case for this?

Armed with a new view of talent the next question is: where can it be found? How can talent be developed? What is its character and what does it look like? These questions are the focus of the next chapter.

Chapter 3

Talent Diversity: You Need to Believe It to See It

To succeed we must stop being so goddamn normal. If we behave like all the others, we will see the same things, come up with similar ideas and develop identical products and services ... The only thing more difficult than learning to exploit the last taboo of emotion and imagination is learning to thrive without it. So people and organizations of the world – come out. Or you will be carried out.

Jonas Ridderstrale and Kjell Nordstrom, *Funky Business*, p. 245

The link between talent and diversity

As we have already discussed, organizational survival hinges on being distinctive. Whatever the industry or sector this means standing out, being the first place people turn to, or simply being the first. Organizations achieve distinctiveness by having a real understanding of difference and how it can benefit them. This is about more than simply how they invent or market a new product: it's about their capacity to anticipate opportunities and then adapt to meet them. Successful enterprises understand that being different requires a culture where what's accepted as normal is routinely challenged and where innovation is a prized organizational value. Achieving this requires a supply of talent with a mix of background, ability and perspectives. Perhaps most importantly, it requires leaders who can earn the trust of this workforce knowing when and how to deploy their diversity.

We believe that we need a more sophisticated view of diversity, one that moves beyond compliance and equal opportunities monitoring. Putting new rules on top of a system that is based on a uniform view of success will not improve diversity. We need to understand better why diversity is so important and how it interconnects with the business priorities. When he set off on his journey to turn IBM from the manufacturer to the services company we know today, Lou Gerstner famously said: 'I don't have a diversity strategy, my strategy is diversity'. He was clear that he would need to build the organization's capacity for innovation and responsiveness to its markets.

Think carefully about the main points of talent management and ask yourself these questions: to what extent do these encourage differences in the organization? How well have leadership assessment systems resulted in a more diverse group of board directors? How pluralistic is the model of work and success in your organization? And, when a line manager thinks about 'what talent is' are they really looking for people who look like them?

Meritocracy and diversity – sources of talent

The early pioneers of the talent movement painted a picture of a future where meritocracy reigned. Performance would be the benchmark, potential the differentiator and a common set of corporate competencies would provide an objective reference point against which these things were to be judged. The promise was (and is) alluring. It feels fair, it can be measured and, of course, what gets measured gets done.

Despite this, the more effective we become at assessing competence, the tougher we manage performance; the more we spend on training, and still executives complain that 'we still don't have enough talent'. Moreover, many organizations continue to struggle with the fact that the 'talent' they see always looks and acts the same. This situation is absurd, because it is happening at a time when the labour markets across the West are more diverse than ever. We have considered this through a gender perspective but we could have also looked at ethnicity, disability, sexual orientation or age and the story would have remained the same. Labour markets are being transformed through immigration, demographic shifts and economic fragmentation.

In the East the picture is different but no less dramatic. India's middle class is soaring to 40% of the population, raising educational standards and career expectations to unprecedented levels. China continues growing at 8–10% annually, year on year, trebling its graduates in five years and producing 6.5 million graduates in 2009. Both countries are moving away from an over-reliance on a mixed ex-patriate pipeline, working instead to rapidly strengthen the capability of home-grown talent. Interestingly, despite very different circumstances the East, like the West, also needs to meet the challenges of homogeneity and start genuinely welcoming differences inside its workforce.

Sociologists tell us that diversity is now much more than where we come from and our biology. It's about our 'biography', when we were born, how we live and who we aspire to be. These extend the Y, X and Boomer generations into another dimension. These groups are criss-crossed by many other social tribes. These tribes are springing up across continents and add more complexity to how talent can be realized in organizations. Perhaps the most significant drivers for these tribes worldwide are technology, education and poverty.

Today's sixteen-year-olds are about to join the workforce. Born in the 1990s, they have grown up with increased convergence in technology and the way we communicate. These 'Millennials' have grown up with on-line social networking, fantasy gaming, blogging, video conversation, instant messaging and interactive TV. They are developing different forms of language and ways of communicating with each other. These forms of communication are vastly different to the narrow forms of communicating in organizations today. This also adds a fourth generation into the workforce, greatly complicating how the employment proposition gets organized.

This latest workforce generation has also had unprecedented access to education and yet there is some evidence to suggest that in the West, while qualification standards are rising, skill levels are falling. This drop in skill levels appears to have been driven by the emphasis on passing exams and increasing participating in higher education. Employers complain that despite the increased supply of graduates the quality of recruits has dropped. At the opposite end of the spectrum, school leavers are short on basic skills and vocational training. The unlucky people at the bottom of the chain are facing lengthy unemployment (and further deskilling) as future waves of graduates and economic migrants enter the market.

The size of the US, Indian and Chinese labour markets means that they continue to have a sufficient mix of skills to satisfy the changing demands of their economies. Sadly, the presence of social poverty may prove to have the biggest impact on the supply of talent worldwide. It is now estimated that our societies operate on a two-thirds principle, where there is always one-third of society 'left behind'. The fall-out of this into communities, crime, inequality and social exclusion is well documented. At the global level, the Southern hemisphere continues to trail the North in terms of wealth. On this stage the wealthiest 20% of humanity consumes 80% of its resources.

We believe that today's talent pools are dangerously homogenous. What we mean by this is that the leadership of our organizations has become over-reliant on people who share similar backgrounds and aspirations. This produces an over-reliance on a narrow set of skills and a worldview that works well in familiar conditions but leaves the organization exposed to changes and future challenges.

The reason why at the macro level poverty is so damaging to our talent supply is because it has a multiplier effect on skill levels, health and life chances. These diminish the size and quality of the talent supply at all levels. This potential loss of up to a third of society entering the labour market, coupled with a projected shortfall in the active workforce by 2040, will lead to increased talent shortages.

Boiled frogs and Chilean potatoes ... why diversity is vital

These are unprecedented times. On both sides of the world different generations and cultures live, work and consume alongside each other. It is a social kaleidoscope that, despite looming shortages, offers an unprecedented opportunity to strengthen the talent pipeline and build the organization's capacity for distinctiveness.

When you look at the picture this way, there is a view that says 'let nature take its course – if society is changing, this must surely filter into the workforce and then up through the talent pipeline, right?' Well perhaps in time this will prove to be true, however, this could take a generation (at least).

Waiting for this to occur 'naturally' is simply not an option for many organizations that already face the challenges of different patterns of consumer demand, or unforeseen demand in public services. We believe that today's talent pools are dangerously homogenous. What we mean by this is that the leadership of our organizations has become over-reliant on people who share similar backgrounds and aspirations. This produces an over-reliance on a narrow set of skills and a worldview that works well in familiar conditions but leaves the organization exposed to changes in environmental conditions. This is a little like Charles Handy's famous parable of the 'Boiled Frog', where the unfortunate amphibian exists happily in an increasingly warm pot, so much so that it fails to notice the subtle increases of temperature even when it is too late ...

It seems likely that we have been living through a period where our HR practices have actively selected and developed people towards a uniform idea of success. Consider the ubiquitous competency framework. These describe the skills and knowledge required to perform in a role or progress through the organization. They are beloved of HR practitioners because they have the potential to articulate what the organization expects of people and to join up different elements of the HR service chain. For example, if Company X has a set of leadership competencies that values 'Burning Drive, Influencing Others and Delivering Results' as the essential characteristics of its leaders, it will then recruit, assess, promote, educate and reward on this basis. Those not demonstrating these characteristics will be managed towards these, or simply managed out. These characteristics will then be applied to its graduate recruitment and then each stage of the management career path. Success in this organization will be awarded to those who best exemplify these qualities and the succession plan will be adjusted accordingly. In time, the whole of its leadership cadre will reflect these competencies and Company X will be known and respected for these qualities.

We have been living through a period where our HR practices have actively selected and developed people towards a uniform idea of success.

From a management perspective this sounds like a success story. We have clarity, we have a common reference point and we have conformity – which of course makes everything much easier to manage. Looking at this from a systems perspective, however, suggests that this conformity has dangerous consequences damaging economic success and the ability to adapt as well as narrowing the supply of vital talent. The true story of the Chilean potato farmer (told by Arie De Geus on page 149 of *The Living Company*, published by Harvard Business Publishing, 2002), tells why diversity in its simplest form is essential for survival.

> Chilean peasants, based all their life in the mountains, know that a wide variety of terrible things can harm their potatoes. There may be a late night frost, or a caterpillar plague. Mildew might destroy plants before the tubers are formed, or winter might come early. Over the years, each of these calamities has taken place. Whenever a new calamity strikes, the peasants walk up to their fields and look everywhere for the surviving plants; only these are immune to the latest plague. At harvesting time they carefully dig up the survivors and take the precious tubers back to their huts. They and their children may have to go through a winter of famine, but at least they have next years seed potatoes from which a new start can be made. They are not locked into any particular set of farming practices, or a particular type of potato; they may be inefficient at times, but they have diversity bred into their everyday practice, diversity that allows them to meet unforeseen disaster.

Diversity – the best way to future-proof your business and avoid homogeneity

A lack of diversity not only exposes the organization, it damages economic success. Competencies such as those in Company X will be based on the personal experiences of its current leadership team and the demands of the current business environment. These personal views while relevant are based on each individual executive's personal success formula. This will have been based on the actions they took which got rewarded, the role models they looked to, their wins and also their war stories. These experiences, while important, will be drawn from a different age. Think about it: many of today's senior executives were building their careers in the 1980s (some even earlier), when society and success looked very different. These formative years will have established deep patterns of behaviour and unconscious preferences that help them make decisions today. This tendency is natural and necessary for all of us and essential for us to function as individuals. At the company level however, hardwiring these experience into the organizational 'DNA' will establish a prevailing culture of success that is highly homogenous and easily dated.

A recent McKinsey study into the career patterns of women leaders identified this homogenized culture as the most important barrier to women's progression. McKinsey described Western attitudes to work as being based on a model of performance characterized by masculine attributes. This model emphasizes the importance of upward mobility, outspoken opinion and confident self-promotion. These traits are complemented by a work culture driven by competition and long hours, where in many cases family is subservient to career. This has become known as the 'double burden syndrome', where women have the greater tendency to take work and domestic responsibilities. Success for women in these workplaces means conforming to this performance code. The McKinsey research suggests that many women are opting out of these environments, not because they are unable to work in this way but simply because they don't want to. In a study published by the *Harvard Business Review* of US college graduates, 37% of women take career breaks, compared to 24% of men. Those women who do stay become adept at working these codes and make life choices accordingly. Significantly, 49% of the highest paid women are childless compared with only 19% of their male equivalents.

This same study has discovered that those organizations with more women in key positions reported a higher profitability than their counterparts. Those with three women or more on the managing committee had operating margins and market capitalization at least twice as high as their lowest ranked counterparts. It is tempting to conclude that this difference may simply be the result of superior ability! The real reason, however, appears to be related to the perspective women bring to the governance and the operation of the organization. This suggests that it isn't the fact that these companies have women at senior levels that makes them more successful: it is because they have a mix of men and women.

Perhaps most significantly, an increased presence of women in senior positions improves the organization's capacity to anticipate and tap into changing patterns of consumption. It is estimated that in Europe women are now behind 70% of all household-purchasing decisions. In the USA, women lead 83% of consumption choices. In Japan, women influence 60% of car sales, while in the UK, the combined purchasing power of the over 55s, disabled, lesbian and gay market accounts for some £300 billion of expenditure.

No surprise then that Stonewall, the UK's leading charity for lesbian, gay and bisexual (LGB) equality now has over 500 corporate members who are committed to developing workplaces where people can be themselves. To many employers this makes commercial sense, since 55% of UK's LGB population report that workplace discrimination negatively impacts on their work. Stonewall's research has also demonstrated a link to organization reputation and employment brand. Seventy-four per cent of gay and 42% of straight consumers are less likely to be associated with organizations that hold a negative view of gay people. Stonewall undertakes an annual, Workplace Equality Index (copyright Stonewall) to benchmark the practice of participating employers. IBM achieved first place (for the second time in the index's six-year history) and deploys a sophisticated perspective on how LGB colleagues bring value to its business. They were one of the few businesses to make the connection to their external relationships; in particular suppliers and prospective employees. IBM UK and Ireland CEO, Brendon Riley comments:

> In 2009 we celebrated the 25th anniversary of IBM's global LGB non-discrimination policy – but we are constantly looking for new ways to enrich and broaden the scope of what we can achieve. We've looked more closely at the LGB network group, its value proposition and its lifecycle – to ensure it continues to deliver value. We've also begun enhanced career monitoring to ensure LGB colleagues are being treated equally in career development and promotion opportunities, and to build a pipeline of future executives. To this end we have established a LGB Executive Forum sponsored by IBM, to share best practice between organizations and support others to establish effective and pervasive equality agendas. Diversity constitutes our character, our identity and ultimately our success – it is in our DNA.

The conclusion is that a more flexible way of working will attract more diversity into the talent pipeline. We suspect that this issue relates to issues of ethnicity, age and disability as much as LGB. IBM's success also demonstrates the value of actively targeting different sectors and monitoring progress. Increasing diversity across the leadership population increases the organization's capacity to understand and respond to the external environment and its customers.

A new war for talent

When you think about it, there is something a little odd about building a talent pipeline that conforms to a set of competencies based on thinking from yesteryear. This is a mindset that says 'talent must fit the organization and its ways'. Alright, we have a diminishing labour market, skills are in short supply, four generations want to work in different ways, and only the junior levels of the workforce reflect the changing social mix, and we still adhere to the principle that talent must work around us…

Is it any wonder we have a 'War for Talent'? Despite the recent economic downturn talented individuals, those who have the ability to help our organizations thrive, can call the shots. They choose to stay, to leave or simply to switch off. And yet we create 'talent' activities that ask them to conform to a very singular notion of success, jump through assessment hoops, and we push them towards roles that take them away from home. We also tell too many of them that despite their vital contribution they 'lack potential'. That is, of course if we tell them at all, since so much talent activity continues in secret. This is breathtaking arrogance. It is hardly surprising that the issue of retention has now suddenly become such a vital preoccupation.

When you look at the problem this way we believe that there is a new War for Talent and it is inside the organization itself. If we are to retain and realize the capacity of talented people we need a more pluralistic view of what talent is. We also need to rebuild our organization's cultural codes; our heroes need to look different. Imagine if we could build an organization based on the range of capability and potential that everyone brought in the door, not just on those capabilities we were looking for at the time. People have more talent than they realize and it is only a lack belief that gets in the way.

Practical actions that will begin making a difference

There are several practical actions that can make a difference immediately.

    1.   **Integrate talent, diversity and organization strategies.** Lack of diversity is a sophisticated issue that requires a sophisticated response. Thinking of diversity as an employment or a compliance issue or as an end in itself is unlikely to impact on the talent agenda. Think instead of diversity as a vehicle for improving the talent supply. Consider how widening participation in talent schemes can provide a better understanding of the type of insight and skills mix required to deliver the business strategy.

Be clear about the capability required to drive future success. How will market share be widened, which consumers will be making purchasing decisions? What communities will the organization be reaching into? How much innovation will be required and in what areas? What are the ambitions for the Brand and the related customer experience? Dig deep into the segmentation profiles and customer experience data provided by the marketing teams. Sit in on focus groups and product or service observations. Look out for changes in consumer behaviour and any un-met needs. These will provide insights into the type of capability and structure required to meet these needs.

Once this is established, review the type of talent required and the critical roles that will be needed. Consider how under-represented groups can contribute to this and articulate a case for senior leaders to understand why this is a valuable thing. Develop robust information on the demographic character of the current organization and identify indicators to chart progress.

Take care not to simply reprize the moral argument. Stay focused instead on demonstrating the link between widening participation and results.

    2.   **Identify the 'DNA' of the organization.** This is always a sensitive activity since it involves holding a mirror up to the existing executive team and asking them to reflect on how their leadership style helps and hinders the strategy.

Talk to external stakeholders, customers and employees from across all key constituencies about the underpinning character operating inside the organization. Use employee engagement data if you have this. Explore the pros and cons of this 'DNA' in relation to organizational objectives, competitor behaviour and brand promise. Will continuing in this vein help or hinder the progress of the organization? What's missing in the character that will undermine how the organization will respond to its environment?

Compare and contrast the profiles of the leadership team and how these drive the organizational culture. To what extent do the team conform to a uniform behavioural type? Are their strengths biased to a small number of key areas, if so what are the risks? Alternatively is there room for each individual 'signature' and how do these differences manifest themselves?

This diagnostic approach should lead to a conversation about the character of the culture which needs to change to better reflect the organization's priorities. Take care to avoid defining a uniform style that will encourage homogeneity. Consider instead those characteristics which will encourage diversity, continual learning and innovation. You should aim to articulate:

- What it means to perform well (and also to under-perform) and how this is rewarded.
- What success looks like and how it gets recognized.
- What talent is (also what it isn't) and what it gets in relation to everyone else.
- How communication will happen and how employee feedback is auctioned.
- The degree of flexibility available in work patterns and in careers.
- The organizational values that guide what is and what is not acceptable.

Ensure that you check back with key constituencies (not just the executive team). This will widen the employment proposition to better reflect the needs of under-represented groups.

3. **Develop a dedicated career development approach for under-represented groups.** Research shows that successful careers are based on ability, a strong sense of personal purpose and an ability to learn and adapt and capability to effectively navigate organizational politics. Under-represented groups need focused guidance on how to develop in these areas.

Increasingly leading organizations are creating space for female, black and lesbian and gay colleagues to develop these skills in dedicated groups. This can take the form of breakfast sessions, network groups and even dedicated cohort based development programmes. Whatever the format, the most successful benefit comes from senior sponsorship and professional facilitation to help them get off the ground.

Mentoring plays a key role in helping individuals gain insight into how senior leaders operate. It also provides important visibility of an individual's capability and potential at more senior levels. This visibility keeps them more front of mind and better placed to hear about forthcoming vacancies and project opportunities. Mentors need to dispense encouraging and realistic advice, particularly when an individual's view of their own potential might not match their current capability.

It is also important to recognize the successful individuals from these groups as role models and to structure leadership development and executive education programmes. Increasingly innovation teams invite these individuals into working groups to trial new products and services. We would actively encourage all opportunities to keep development real and action centred.

Finally, it is important to build a sustainable approach into your development of diverse talent. These role models should be actively involved in the recruitment and mentoring of colleagues at more junior levels in the organization.

Leadership reflections

Surely to truly realize the benefits of all its talent, an organization should seek to mould itself more to the talent available to it, not the other way around? Consider how it is that so many of our practices focus on how people fit and what they lack. When did we last look at the whole workforce and ask 'What talents do we have, where are our unique strengths and how can we play to these?' As leaders we would ask you to look deeply at the character of your organizations and the type of talent ecology that is created.

Consider the following questions:

1. To what extent does your business strategy acknowledge the increasing diversity of the market's social base?
2. How is performance judged and rewarded?
3. What does success mean and how do you recognize it?
4. What do you look for in a new recruit? (To what extent does this reflect the characteristics of your current leadership population?)
5. Who does the hiring and where do you go to hire?
6. Who gets developed and access to senior mentors?
7. How many risks do you take on promotions – do you wait for people to be fully competent or stretch into role?
8. What happens when people don't fit into the team?
9. What type of work patterns are acceptable? How easy is it for employees to take a career break and then come back?
10. When (as a leader) did you last take on board a challenge from your team?

These ten questions ask you to look at the norms of behaviour in relation to who stays and rises through the organization. We know that many organizations have an unwritten code for 'what it means to be successful here'. In retailing it's about 'running stores', in banking it's about 'dealing with big customers', in health it's about 'clinical presence', in telecoms it's about 'network reliability'. You won't find *it* in the staff handbook or in the HR competence framework. You will see it in how your colleagues make decisions about people, what they value and what they don't, and how they work. Listen to the way people comment on successful people, to the attributes that get noticed, and the frequency with which they are mentioned.

The need for a practical, business edge to the way that people are managed and led is the focus of the next chapter: strategy.

Chapter 4

Strategy – Beginning With the End in Mind

The strategist's method is very simply to challenge the prevailing assumptions with a single question: Why?

Kenichi Ohmae, *The Mind of the Strategist*, Mcgraw-Hill

Strategies succeed by being as simple and compelling as possible, routinely guiding decisions. They are considered and relevant as well as aspirational; they are distinctive, sometimes bold and audacious, and they play to a firm's strengths, now and in the future.

One day, the chief HR officer will be seated at the same table as other business leaders. Before that happens, however, those other leaders will need to recognize and value the work of people management professionals as being central to the strategy, future and success of their organization. Unfortunately, for too long now people management professionals in many enterprises have been undervalued. This confused situation makes the claim that 'people are our most valuable resource' sound particularly hollow. The truth is that people issues underpin every other aspect of an organization's activities: they are essential for any organization to implement a strategy, serve customers, innovate or simply generate revenue profits and value. The problem is complex: too often HR practices are disconnected or peripheral to the business strategy, and it can appear as if HR professionals are concerned about people at the expense of other priorities (such as profitability, serving customers or creating value). The link between HR and business strategy is just not clear enough.

Views of HR are changing, but a 2003 survey of 1,310 organizations by the Corporate Research Forum highlighted the following views of HR's involvement in business strategy:

- 63% of respondents said HR understands strategic direction, compared with 89% of senior managers and 66% of middle managers;
- less than 30% of respondents believed HR's strategic priorities were shaped by business strategy – and just 23% had a fully integrated planning process between the business and HR;
- only 53% of the senior HR team are involved in developing their organization's strategic plan (47% in its review and 21% in plan approval).

Given this data it's surprising that HR professionals make any headway at all, with relatively few represented at board level and even fewer going on to become Chief Executives of their organizations. As we pointed out earlier, managing people and specifically managing those who we regard as 'talent' has become fiercely complex and for relatively little gain or benefit. This situation is not helping people or their organizations *enough*, and there is an opportunity cost too: strategies are being frustrated because people are spending too many resources doing too many things that have only limited or peripheral value, at best. Meanwhile, vitally important issues and facts are being neglected.

The truths about talent highlight why people management issues are so important. Remember:

- we are all talent now;
- talent is abundant and diverse;
- the talented are those who generate value, not merely those who can get to the top;
- potential is discretionary;
- growing and engaging talent is at the core of leadership;
- HR must reinvent itself to deliver practices for a 'workforce of one';
- talented people are attracted to talented places.

Given this situation, HR professionals have really only one priority: making sure that an organization's employees and their leaders are doing all that they can to support the business strategy.

Strategy – the first priority

'Talent strategy' and 'People strategy' need to be entirely in service of the overall strategy of the business. If that truth is accepted, it follows that HR professionals should be intimately involved in developing and implementing the strategy. The priority, therefore, is to make explicit the fundamental (and obvious) link between people management strategy and tactics on one side, and the overall business strategy. There are several ways that this can be achieved:

- future thinking;
- strategy development;
- strategy implementation;
- communication.

First, it is vital to understand what is meant by strategy: a concept that is over-used and frequently misunderstood. Business strategy can be defined simply as the plans, choices and decisions used to guide a business to greater profitability and success. A successful strategy distinguishes a business and provides the impetus for commercial success.

One issue that lies at the heart of business strategy is choice. Strategy business has three essential elements: development, implementation and selling (meaning, obtaining commitment and buy-in). Underpinning all three is choice, in particular the need to choose a distinctive strategic position about:

- Who to target as customers (and who to avoid targeting).
- What products to offer.
- How to undertake related activities efficiently.

Strategy is all about making tough choices in these three areas. It means deciding on the customers you will target and, just as important, the customers you will not target. This requires a focus on customers, segmenting in ways that are most useful and productive. Delivering a successful strategy also means choosing the products or services you will offer and what product features or benefits to emphasize. Finally, strategy means choosing the right activities to sell your selected product to your selected customer.

In every industry there are several viable positions that a company can occupy. The essence of strategy therefore is to choose the one position that your company will claim as its own. A strategic position is simply the sum of a business's answers to the three issues mentioned above: who will we target, what will we offer and how will success be ensured? The goal for every business should be to answer these questions differently from its competitors. If you can do that, your business can stake out a unique strategic position.

Future thinking and scenarios

Why future thinking and scenarios are valuable

For employees, a business strategy provides a guiding view of the future that influences their decisions, priorities and way of working. People generally like to do work that is meaningful or at least purposeful. Strategy provides that purpose. In this way it helps to give individual fulfilment. This psychological element points to an important and rarely considered point about strategy: the intangible and valuable contribution it makes to employees' commitment, engagement, productivity, creativity and success. Simply put, people work better and achieve more if they believe in what they are doing and have confidence in the direction they are going. Conversely, uncertainty or insecurity about the future breeds tension, lack of confidence and even cynicism, none of which are conducive to business success or personal achievement. Finally for individuals, a sound strategy leads individuals to develop their personal potential and, invariably, to attain new skills. This then initiates a self-sustaining cycle of confidence, self-awareness and success.

A vital role for HR working with everyone in the organization (the abundant supply of talent) is future thinking. It is especially valuable for helping to analyse a situation, understand the priorities and make the right decisions for the future.

For shareholders, strategy also provides a way of measuring the business's progress. Events may obscure the reality of a firm's short-term performance, but what cannot be obscured is whether the right strategy and direction have been chosen, and the progress made in fulfilling that strategy.

Scenarios help managers to tackle risk, uncertainty and complexity. Scenario planning enables businesses to rehearse the future, to walk the battlefield before battle commences, if you like, so that they're better prepared. Its value lies not in predicting the future, but in enabling business owners and managers to recognize and understand future developments, and thereby to influence events.

Scenario thinking has been used by the military for centuries and by organizations such as Royal Dutch/Shell since the 1960s. According to Kees van der Heijden, formerly Professor of Strategy at Strathclyde Graduate School of Business: 'Scenario planning is neither an episodic activity nor a new technique: it is a way of thinking that works best when it permeates the entire organization, affecting decisions at all levels. However, unlike most popular management initiatives, it does not require major investment in resources or restructuring, simply a commitment for people to take time away from their routine activities to come together to reflect and learn'.

A vital role for HR working with everyone in the organization (the abundant supply of talent) is *future thinking*. It is especially valuable for helping to analyse a situation, understand the priorities and make the right decisions for the future. Scenarios are perspectives on potential events and their consequences, and they provide a context in which managers can make decisions. By thinking through a range of possible future scenarios, decisions are better informed. In turn, any strategies based on this deeper insight are more likely to succeed. HR has a valuable role to play in creating the conditions where managers in particular can think about the future: what may happen and how the business can benefit from their work.

HR needs to help employees and their organizations realize the benefits of scenarios. These benefits include:

• **Generating greater understanding of present circumstances, likely developments and future possibilities.** Scenario thinking helps to provide a better understanding of how different factors affecting a business affect each other. It can reveal links between apparently unrelated factors, and, most importantly, it can provide greater insight into the forces shaping the future, and in so doing can deliver real competitive advantage.

- **Helping to overcome complacency.** Scenarios should be designed to challenge established views and 'same old, same old' thinking so that new ideas can be tried out. Seeing reality from different perspectives should really shake things up and stop people passing the buck.
- **Emphasizing action and 'ownership'.** Scenario thinking helps to break the constraints of traditional practices, as it enables those involved to discuss the complexity and ambiguity of their perspectives in a wide context.
- **Stimulating creativity and innovation.** Scenarios encourage people to open up their minds to new possibilities and the excitement of how they may be realized. The process leads to a positive attitude that actively seeks the desired outcome.
- **Promoting learning.** Scenarios help people to understand their environment, consider the future, share knowledge and evaluate strategic options.
- **Creating a 'shared view'.** Scenario thinking works because it looks beyond current assignments, facts and forecasts. It allows discussions to be more uninhibited and it creates the conditions for an effective, shared sense of purpose to evolve. To make sure that new ideas aren't strangled at birth, make sure that all the key decision-makers in your company are involved. If you're a sole trader, ask trusted friends or advisors to help you out here.

There are two things that we can say for certain about the future: it will be different and it will surprise. Despite this simple fact and the benefits of scenarios and future thinking mentioned above, people, businesses, organizations – even whole societies – are constantly caught out by their failure to anticipate, prepare for and respond to far-reaching changes. We often hear that 'Change is the only constant' but we invariably behave as if no change is the only constant and the status quo rules supreme. So, why is this and what can be done?

A friend recently told us a revealing story that shows how valuable the role of HR could be when it comes to strategy in general and future thinking in particular. She commutes to London by train and currently the service is drastically reduced because the company is short of drivers (the company relied on drivers working overtime, which very few are now prepared to do). It takes a year to train a driver so unless the firm increases overtime rates, which it is unwilling or unable to contemplate, there is no quick fix: this is a long-term problem.

In a factsheet published with a temporary timetable, the company says: 'The situation has developed into significant disruption, as a growing number of individuals increasingly withdrew from working rest days and overtime. In hindsight, perhaps we should have assumed worse-case scenario from the beginning. We apologize that the message we have communicated to you has fallen short and our reaction to unfolding events may have seemed reactive rather than proactive.'

The reaction of their customers, including our friend, is yes: you really should have assumed a worse-case scenario and you're right – a little more proactivity would have been good. It's tempting to think of this situation either as a simple mistake (the benign view) or unbelievable folly (the harsher view). The sad truth is that many firms often make these types of mistake. In fact, the root causes are often the same and, encouragingly, so are the solutions.

The problem is that we often fail to think deeply enough about how the world is changing. We understand and can see that the world is changing all the time but, because we are so focused and because change is so ubiquitous, we fail to think deeply enough about the implications. To illustrate this point, consider a few simple facts. Around the year 1800, global population reached 1 billion; by 1900, it was 1.6 billion; by 2000, it had reached 6.1 billion (global population actually doubled between the administrations of Presidents Kennedy and Clinton). Current world population is approximately 6.9 billion and set to plateau at around 9 billion by the middle of the century. This is fascinating but it is the implications of this change that matter most. More people are living longer, with consequences for markets, products, innovation, employment, skills, leadership and a range of other issues. There is more migration, so everything from the supply of skills to cross-border trade alters; there is more urbanization, so the incidence of business-disrupting plagues such as SARS increases alongside commercial opportunities. And so on.

Too often, we see the change but fail to appreciate the implications. For example, we can say today that, barring an unprecedented global catastrophe, there will be around 2.2 billion people over the age of 65 alive in 2050. This isn't guesswork: all of those people are alive today. The point is that predicting the future isn't the challenge: understanding it is.

So, what does this have to do with our friend waiting for her train? I believe her train company's predicament is shared by thousands of other businesses. They believe the past is a guide to the future and they fail to see how the world is shifting (in this case, the attitude of the train drivers). This simple fact has caught out many leading businesses including: Lehman Brothers, Woolworths, MFI, Kodak, General Motors, Daewoo and others. In most of these cases, complacency and a commitment to the status quo escalated in a smooth, undisturbed fashion. The danger is that lack of awareness and connection to the outside world will increase gradually, incrementally and almost imperceptibly. This simple fact provides the foundation for most business difficulties. Firms that declined or failed simply did not do enough to understand or prepare for the future during the good times. In retrospect, countless executives recognize that good is the enemy of great – meaning their firms were doing well so they saw no reason to change. By the time they came to realize that the world around them had changed (notably customers, competitors, regulators and – in the case of my friend's train company – their employees) it was too late to respond.

Learning from the past, preparing for the future

Given the typical situation facing our friend's rail company, two questions dominate: what are the lessons from the past and present? How is corporate success sustained? There is, of course, a fortune to be made (or, at least, not lost) for the person who answers these questions, so unsurprisingly many have tried. The best answers appear consistently and they lie at the heart of scenario planning.

• **Use scenarios.** Scenarios are not about predicting events but understanding the forces shaping the future. The priority is to explore potential situations and options. They help firms to recognize opportunities, assess options and take decisions.

- **Avoid active inertia.** Donald Sull, author of *Revival of the Fittest*, believes managers get trapped by success, a condition he calls active inertia. This is when managers respond to disruptive changes by accelerating activities that succeeded in the past, often simply digging themselves further into a hole. Active inertia is overcome by focusing on new goals and priorities.

- **Understand the limits of your success.** Managers become used to operating with a formula that is familiar and has achieved success. However, when the situation alters (a global recession arrives or train drivers get restive) then strengths become weaknesses and assets become liabilities.

- **Avoid dramatic change.** Jim Collins, best-selling author of *Good to Great*, argues that dramatic changes and restructurings may save the day but they do little to develop success. What matters is sustained, cumulative progress and change.

- **Keep it real and confront the honest truth.** When considering the causes of change, we see people unable to understand or adapt to change. In retrospect, people identify changes that passed unnoticed at the time. Typical examples include new products and new substitutes arriving or changes in technology and markets.

Above all, look to understand the future. Surprisingly, few businesses seem to do this – even now – which of course is an opportunity for those that do.

Checklist: using scenario thinking

The effectiveness of scenario thinking lies in stimulating decisions, in what is often called a 'strategic conversation'. This is the continuous process of planning, analysing the environment, generating and testing scenarios, developing options, selecting, refining and implementing, a process that is itself refined by further environmental analysis.

1. **Plan and structure the scenario process.** First of all, identify gaps in organizational knowledge that relate to business challenges whose impact on the organization is uncertain. To do this, create a team to plan and structure the process. Ideally, team members should probably come from outside the organization for some objectivity. The best people for this type of role should be creative thinkers who are comfortable challenging

conventional ideas. In discussion with the team, decide on the duration of the project; ten weeks is considered appropriate for a big project.

2.   Understand the business context. Interview team members to assess their main views and to work out whether these ideas are shared by different team members. Focus on vital issues such as:

- What customers value.
- The previous success formula.
- Future challenges.

Identify how each individual views the past, present and future aspects of each issue. The interview statements should be collated and analysed in an interview report, structured around the recurring concepts and key themes. This now sets the agenda for the first workshop and should be sent to all participants. As a starting point for the workshop, it is also valuable to identify the critical uncertainties and issues as perceived by the participants.

3.   Develop the scenarios. The workshop should identify the forces that will have an impact over an agreed period. Two possible opposite outcomes should be agreed, and the forces that could lead to each of them should be listed. This will help to show how these forces link together. Next, decide whether each of these forces has a low or high impact and a low or high probability. This information should be displayed on a 2 × 2 matrix.

By having two polar outcomes and all the driving forces clearly presented, the team can then develop the likely 'histories', or scenarios, that led to each outcome. These histories of the future can then be expanded through discussion of the forces behind the changes. The aim is not to develop accurate predictions; it is to understand what will shape the future and how different events interact and influence each other. All the time, discussions are focused on each scenario's impact on the organization.

This part of the process opens up the thinking of the members of the team and it alerts them to signals that may suggest a particular direction for the organization. The outcomes of different responses are 'tested' in the safety of scenario planning, avoiding the risks of real implementation.

4.   Analyse the scenarios. The analysis stage examines the external issues and internal logic. Consider:

- What are the priorities and concerns of those outside the organization?
- Who are the key players? Do they change and what do they want?
- What would they want to see? What would they think of your current situation?

Systems and process diagrams can help to address these questions, as can discussions with other stakeholders. Remember, we are not trying to pinpoint future events but to consider the forces that may push the future along different paths.

5.   Use the scenarios. This means:

- Working backwards from the future to the present – the team should formulate an action plan that can influence the organization's thinking.
- Identifying the early signs of change so that when they do occur, they will be recognized and responded to quickly and effectively.
- Continuing the process by identifying gaps in understanding and organizational knowledge.

The participatory and creative process sensitizes managers to the outside world. It helps individuals and teams to recognize the uncertainties in their operating environments, so that they can question their everyday assumptions, adjust their mental maps and think 'outside the box'.

6.   Avoid problems. People who work with scenarios find it to be exciting, valuable and enjoyable. It can also lead to a tangible and significant result: a shift in attitude, as well as greater certainty, confidence and understanding. Do bear in mind that some problems can arise, though:

- Misunderstanding what it is that the scenarios are intended to achieve: scenarios are not predictions; they are a guide to understanding what possible futures lie ahead and what forces may be at work, now and in the future, to make these futures a reality.

- Failing to create or explore scenarios that are either viable or sufficiently imaginative: too often people rely on in-house views, traditional perceptions and internal problems; the resulting scenarios are then too narrowly focused or close to home.
- Failing to adopt a rigorous, intelligent and informed approach: scenario planning begins with deep and thorough analysis and understanding of the present.
- Ignoring, downgrading or simply failing to act on the scenarios: make sure that scenarios are rigorous, and give them status, for example, by off-site meetings, high-level sponsors and management feedback. Also, use the scenarios to drive decision-making by stimulating debate. They should be used to develop strategy, test business or project plans and manage risk.
- Failing to communicate the scenario, with the result that it does not become embedded in thinking or decision-making. Instead, use imaginative and frequent communications to embed scenario-thinking into discussion and decisions.
- Misunderstanding the link between short-term and long-term success and prosperity: if management orients the business towards a successful future, that automatically points the company towards opportunities for enhanced profitability, productivity and customer satisfaction in the short-term. Remember, short-term victories won at the expense of the future inevitably end up as defeats.

Developing strategy

The essence of successful strategies
There are several significant points to note about successful strategies.

They are flexible and adaptable, capable of responding to opportunities and unforeseen challenges. This point was highlighted by one of the world's richest entrepreneurs, Warren Buffett, in his Chairman's letter to Berkshire Hathaway shareholders in their 1999 annual report. In this report he shed light on one of the factors behind Berkshire Hathaway's acquisition strategy – simply waiting for the phone to ring.

He went on to explain that usually it does, because a manager who sold their business to Berkshire earlier is now recommending that one of their friends does the same. The need for flexibility is also highlighted by Robert H. Waterman is his 1994 book *The Frontiers of Excellence*. 'Strategies that succeed are organic. They evolve. They wrap themselves around problems, challenges, and opportunities, make progress and move on' (reproduced by permission of Nicholas Brealey).

They guide the way people work and the decisions they make, now and in the future. Crucially, a strategy is something that has a trajectory, it is dynamic and its future is linked to its past. This point was recognized by Peter Drucker in his 1980 book *Managing in Turbulent Times*. 'Long-range planning does not deal with future decisions. It deals with the future of present decisions' (reproduced by permission of Elsevier).

The great thing about strategy and strategic decisions is that they are the keys to the future. They provide reassurance, overcoming concerns and challenges. They reduce or remove sources of stress. More positively, they turn problems into opportunities – and they can create opportunities and benefits out of very little. Perhaps because of their significance and value, decisions can be demanding, even daunting for many people. Often, we arrive at decisions quickly, subconsciously, without considering our options. For strategy to succeed simple planning, openness and a constructive, enquiring approach goes a long way.

They are an essential, constant guide to developing the business. A business that doesn't use a strategy (or has one that is flawed) is like a traveller that doesn't use a map: the potential for confusion, disappointment and failure increases massively. The fact is that if you don't know where you are going then any road will do.

They focus on customers as the surest route to profitable growth. It is customers that give strategy meaning. Strategist Michael Porter writing in *Harvard Business Review* (November–December 1996) is in broad agreement: 'Competitive strategy is about being different. It means deliberately choosing a different set of activities to deliver a unique mix of values'.

They understand that the journey is as important as the destination, and both the means and the ends are important. The essence of strategy is not only the structure of a company's products and markets but the way it works and the decisions it makes.

Checklist: developing your strategy

Strategic planning has three important phases: analysis, planning and integration.

Analysis. The value of analysis is that it leads to strong conclusions and decisions; it helps you to find the right direction. Analysis needs to be thorough, comprehensive and wide-ranging and to achieve this one technique stands out: questioning. In fact, with strategic analysis there are no good answers, only good questions. That is because strategy is subject to dynamic and constantly shifting forces with the result that the best answers will change over time. The solution, therefore, is to question, decide the best approach, and then check that you are on course with further questioning. In this respect strategy is a little like ocean racing: it requires a clear course but also a constant checking of position, awareness of external forces and a desire to improve.

Analysis creates a wealth of information. The next step is to extract the most valuable parts or those with the greatest effect on your strategy, summarize and share them. A summary of strengths, weaknesses, opportunities and threats is a useful way to analyse this information.

Planning. There are several stages in the strategy planning process, each relying on the completed analysis.

- Defining your purpose – this should summarize where you are now, where you want to be and how you will change.
- Explaining your advantage – people will want to understand how the business will succeed and what success will look like.
- Setting the boundaries for your strategy – it is important to be clear about the products and markets you will deal in, and those you won't. The important point to recognize is that strategy is about making choices and ensuring focus.
- Prioritizing – the strategy needs to emphasize specific products, customers and markets that are the most profitable or significant. Employees

should be given specific responsibilities, objectives and resources so that the potential of these priority areas can be realized.

- Budgeting – recognizing the financial requirement of a strategy is fundamental to its success. The next step, therefore, is to develop a budget that meets the strategic objectives.

These issues should be clearly explained and used to gain people's commitment and focus their attention.

Integration. The strategy needs to take account of the realities of the business. It needs to be consistent with the work of other departments, the capabilities of employees and suppliers, and the expectations of customers. The challenge is to avoid confusion or conflict. This is really a 'sense check' that the strategy will work and it relies on the strategist asking and involving the right people at the right time.

Implementing strategy

There are several other vital aspects of implementing strategy. These include: achieving short-term goals and agreeing clear objectives. As with any major new initiative, achieving quick wins helps to generate momentum, as well as providing practical examples of the strategy in action. Also, objectives should be specific, measurable, achievable, relevant and time-constrained. People also need to be held personally accountable for achieving their objectives. This means setting milestones, agreeing limits of authority and discussing how best to proceed, as well as establishing a system to monitor and measure progress.

The tasks of successfully implementing a strategy vary depending on the industry, organization and strategy, but they typically include:

- Testing aspects of the strategy.
- Coaching people so that they have the required level of skills and confidence.
- Ensuring that people are motivated, engaged and committed to the strategy. For example, reward systems may need to be adjusted to encourage specific actions and behaviours.

- Assessing and monitoring the risks with new initiatives.
- Monitoring performance and reviewing operational targets.

Communicating strategy

The ability to communicate clearly is an essential aspect of implementing a strategy. People need guidance, information, clarity, even reassurance. Leadership is about working productively through others and this cannot be achieved without an ability to communicate. Unfortunately, communication skills are often overlooked. They are so important, so frequently used and so fundamental that they are taken for granted. Leaders frequently overlook the fact that communication skills can always be improved with important benefits for the leader, the team and the success of the organization.

Several techniques can help to develop a leader's skills as a trusted communicator. First, look out for body language – both yours and theirs. Keeping eye contact shows trust and interest, and observing their posture will give some idea of how they feel. Mirroring back someone's body language sensitively is one way of helping to show that you are listening.

Also, asking questions not only improves your understanding but it can also test assumptions and show that you are listening. When asking questions you should also signal for attention: this will let the other person know that you want to comment and respond to their point and allow them to pause and switch their attention to you before you speak. Next, summarize, giving an overview at the start of what you want to say, and finish by summarizing what has been agreed. Summarizing at key intervals helps to prevent misunderstandings and move the conversation on to the next point.

Being critically aware when communicating requires a variety of skills, in particular:

- Reacting to ideas, not people.
- Focusing on the significance of the facts and evidence.
- Avoiding jumping to conclusions.
- Listening for how things are said and what is not said.

When talking to someone you need to be aware of their concerns and reactions, and to achieve this you need to create an honest and open environment. Even then, some people will still not say how they feel or what they think, or they may simply lack the skills to express themselves adequately. In these circumstances the leader needs to ask open, probing questions that will provide an indication of what the person is thinking.

HR strategy at work

This information is valuable for HR professionals who are either developing a strategy for their organization, or supporting the aims of the business with a clearly-focused people strategy. An example of a successful HR strategy is provided by Atlanta-based Southern Company, a major regional utility that is one of America's largest generators of electricity. In this organization, HR's purpose is explicitly linked to the business's strategy and strategic priorities. The HR strategy director works full-time with business leaders, colleagues and line managers to formulate HR strategy for the organization. It has over 25,000 employees and 200 locations. All strategic HR projects have defined goals which are tied to the Strategic Management Process and functional capabilities.

HR's agenda has six priority areas, each of which matches a competitive issue in the US utilities industry: labour costs, organizational efficiency, workforce 'benchstrength' (capability), diversity, leadership effectiveness and developing a high performance culture. The firm believes that their capacity to deliver these priorities is vital for future success – both for the organization and the HR function.

Therefore, HR at Southern Company is aligned with, and responds to, business strategy – but is not part of the strategy formulation team. Its role is in executing strategy. We would argue that HR should be central to business strategy formulation, planning, execution and review – not because the function wants to be or thinks it is 'strategic', but because the business will need it. This involvement and contribution is seen in several areas:

- **Business strategy** – HR provides advantages that support the organization's strategic priorities, differentiate the business and increase competitiveness.
- **HR plans** – these should be integrated with business strategy and the organization's strategic management process, helping to direct attainment of strategic goals.
- **HR results (deliverables)** – these will be determined by what it is the organization needs to accomplish for its future success. These deliverables are the source of HR's value.
- **HR roles and structure** – these will enable HR to execute strategies by focusing its roles on critical issues. Also, HR will create an operating structure that serves the organization by deploying new designs, technology, outsourcing or new operating models.

As a result of their activities in these areas HR will become a ready source of competitive advantage. In the future, business leaders will need reassurance that difficult 'people issues' are being addressed – and will see good execution as the proof that HR deliverables can help resolve these issues. They will need HR that is strategically astute and able to answer key questions:

- Is strategy understood along with its assumptions, goals and implications? Does this understanding routinely guide the way that people work?
- Will HR be able to make informed strategic choices and define the function's strategic challenges?
- Can HR provide new perspectives for non-HR executives on the business model, strategic choices and strategy execution?

Strategic tools for HR

The business case for HR to lead strategy development and implementation is compelling. There are several levers or tools that HR can use to make these changes. The following questions are grouped around these strategic levers and are designed to guide thinking about what the HR function should deliver in the future.

1. Devising the right people strategy

People strategy is distinct from business strategy: it represents the people management and organization dimensions of business strategy.

- What contingencies will this strategy need to cope with? What is the likely response to business uncertainties, surprising 'wild card' events and changes?
- How will business units, functions, work groups, teams and individuals be aligned around the main challenges of this strategy?
- How will you know whether this strategy delivers what is planned?

2. Designing and refining the organization's structure and focus:

- How will you ensure (and satisfy your business leaders) that the organization's core business competencies will remain appropriate for at least the medium term future (the next two to five years)?
- What additional skills and capabilities are envisaged if the business is to continue succeeding?
- What changes to the organization's design and structure are needed?
- How can you improve the organization's ability to manage the major change initiatives and breakthroughs needed?
- What will have to be done to enable you to implement the new ways of operating that future business conditions will require?

3. Influencing and enhancing the culture and environment:

- What will be the defining characteristics of your organization's culture that will set it apart from its competitors?
- What changes to the organization's culture will encourage involvement, commitment and high performance?

- What blockages must be removed to get the culture your organization needs?
- How will you create the conditions and environment to make your organization a great place to work and do business?

4. Developing future leaders

- What kinds of leaders – and in which positions and areas – will be needed to steer the business through different operating conditions over the period of the strategic plan?
- Are current leadership and development plans appropriate for future challenges?
- What will HR have to do about the styles, behaviours and capabilities of future leaders, and how will these changes be achieved?
- How will you improve current resourcing, reward, development, succession planning and performance management for leaders?
- What aspects of board and senior team performance will have to be improved?

5. Understanding critical capabilities

- What will have to be done to improve the capabilities and performance of all employees?
- How will diverse talents, characteristics and cultural differences be managed better to meet the organization's social and legislative obligations?

6. Managing performance and reward

- How will you ensure that, in the future, the best performers are in the right jobs?
- What will you have to do for the organization to become more effective at encouraging and rewarding good performance, and tackling under-performance?

- How will you ensure that performance management at all levels consistently reflects the organization's values and standards as well as actual performance?
- What can be done with rewards and recognition that will help close performance and retention gaps?

7.   Involving people and increasing satisfaction

- How will the organization have to manage its psychological contracts and employer brand differently in the future?
- What future values and sense of purpose will encourage greater employee involvement in your organization's future plans?
- What will have to change to improve people's satisfaction in the future?
- What will you do to build involvement at those times when the company's commitment to employees and employee loyalty lessens?
- Which tools and data give you the most accurate assessments of satisfaction?

8.   Learning and managing knowledge

- How will the organization ensure that learning and development is appropriate and quickly transferred to improve individual or team performance?
- How will technology be used to enable rapid learning, information sharing and knowledge transfer across the enterprise?
- How will the current process and system for managing knowledge be improved to meet future needs?

9.   Staying focused, flexible and managing HR services

- What are the key performance indicators that need to be managed? In particular, which measures for your future view of organizational effectiveness may have to be discarded, adapted or introduced?

- How will HR ensure that complex transactions and administration services for managers and employees are delivered at greatest efficiency and lowest cost?
- What will be the cost-benefits, disadvantages and management issues of shifting to externally provided services through outsourcing?
- How might models such as centralized shared services improve service delivery and enable redeployment of resources elsewhere?
- What future criteria will shape your interpretations of organizational effectiveness?
- How will productivity be continuously improved?
- What changes are needed to current processes to create 'superior performance' in the future?

Leadership reflections

Whether developing a strategy or making strategic decisions, an enquiring, questioning approach is an invaluable place to start. Clearly, this includes questions about the market, customers, innovations, finances, competitors or other business issues – not only the people. One vital point to note, however, is the view that business issues interrelate and connect with each other: it pays to take a systemic view. It is an irony that people are referred to as 'human resources' and then a holistic resource view is often neglected.

So, for example:

- What are the business's most important resources?
- How do your resources interrelate and affect each other?
- Do people have the right skills to move the business where it needs to be?
- Which of your resources are strengthening or accumulating, and which are weakening or draining away?
- How and why will people make your business successfully achieve its goals?

Key Questions

Increasing Awareness and Detecting Warning Signs

- What are the crucial questions facing the business, the questions whose answers imply: 'I wish I had known this five years ago?'
- Are your current attitudes stuck in the mud?
- Are you prepared to accept that a strategy is failing or is vulnerable?
- Is the business in touch with market developments and with what its customers want?
- Are you prepared to try something new?
- Is any part of your business planning weak or unclear?
- Are you confident about your ability to talk about strategy for the business?
- When you make decisions, do you always consider multiple options before deciding? Is the quality of your strategic thinking limited, narrow and uninspired?
- Is your business afraid of uncertainty, or does it enjoy thinking about it? Do people see it as a threat or as an opportunity? Is it viewed as a potential source of competitive advantage?

In his book *The Mind of the Strategist* Japanese management consultant and theorist Kenichi Ohmae explains that 'The strategist's method is very simply to challenge the prevailing assumptions with a single question: Why?'

This chapter has explained how to develop and implement strategy. In the next chapter we look deeper at the issue of implementing strategy, explaining how to create the right conditions for talented people to thrive (the talent ecology) and how to ensure that they – and their organization – achieve their true potential.

Chapter 5

Hire and Wire: Developing Your Organization's Talent Ecology

Once we stop treating organizations and people as machines and stop trying to re-engineer them, once we move into the paradigm of living systems, organizational change is not a problem. Using this new worldview, it is possible to create organizations filled with people who are capable of adapting as needed, who are alert to the changes in the environment, who are able to innovate strategically.

Margaret J Wheatley, We Are All Innovators,
Drucker Foundation Journal, vol 20, 2001

Finding and nurturing talent

History has shown us that talent management has been driven by supply of labour in the external market. When times are good we 'Buy' Talent, injecting fresh perspectives into the organization. There is of course a downside to this, our newcomers take time to make their mark or when they do, their difference is such that the organization rejects them. The cost of this in both personal and financial terms is high. We have both worked in organizations where the turnover in executives during their first year can hit 25%. Disruption, pay offs, search and re-hire fees are sizable, resulting in heavy losses at the corporate level. The cost to the individual is also high, reputation and confidence are shattered with only the most resilient being able to continue on their chosen career path.

When the skills we require are scarce we 'Make' Talent, accelerating the development and progression of those already with us. This too, requires heavy investment in lengthy education programmes or in stretch assignments. Often the individual outgrows their role, and the promised promotion evaporates in the latest restructure. To a capable, ambitious person leaving the organization begins to look like the most attractive way of securing the next opportunity.

Increasingly organizations employ a 'Make and Buy' strategy gingerly treading a tightrope between the risk and benefits. And yet we rarely address the root cause of the risks we are trying to manage. We believe that the success of a Make/Buy strategy is entirely dependent on the character of your organization's *Talent Ecology*. By this we mean the relationship between the individual employee, the talent management activity and the wider organizational system. This system includes the organization's culture, its strategy, structure, its operating habits and the dynamics of the market it sits in. Each of these are interconnected and inter-dependent with each individual employee. An action in one area leads to a reaction in another. How people are welcomed, the stories people tell about success, the way vacancies are communicated, how promotions happen, the way a line manager deals with poor performance, the way work is organized, how employees understand the contribution they make and how people leave, all contribute to a firm's *Talent Ecology*. Every organization has its own Talent Ecology and as highlighted in Chapter 1, this is the 'forest' that 'the tall trees' live in. So, instead of 'Make and Buy' we recommend that you 'Hire & Wire' (a term coined by social network specialist Valdis Krebs in 2000). This builds on the need for just-in-time recruitment and development and adds a third, organizational dimension; how your company is able to sustain talent.

The implications of not doing this can make or break the most sophisticated talent strategy, greatly influencing the risk and return on investment. We also believe that this web of interactions – your social capital, work together to affect the quality talent and performance of your organization whether you are aware of it or not.

Create your organization's talent ecology

Strengthen team ties

Connect to the external market

Make
Innovators
Relationship experts
Change Agents
Networks
Future executives

Buy
Specialist skills
Network & segmentation technologies
Competitive expertise
Interims

Align the culture

Link operating habits

Know every employee

Keep the structure flexible

Link business and talent strategy

Managing your talent ecology

The dictionary definition of 'Ecology' talks of *the study of interaction of persons with their environment*. We have expanded this concept to link in with the talent agenda because we feel it helps explain why conventional approaches to talent management are failing.

As we discussed in Chapter 2, conventional approaches such as annual talent reviews, succession planning and high potential cohort programmes fail to live up to their promise because they are from a different age. In an age where changes were predictable, organizations were less complex and individuals had less to juggle between home and work life. We also believe that conventional approaches fall short because they are process heavy and people light. They fail to recognize the dynamic interplay of individual aspiration and organizational behaviour.

The illustration overleaf details the forces shaping an organization's talent ecology. Each element is inter-connected and dynamic. Often a talent activity is focused only on the process of identifying talent: the capability review, the assessment centres and the succession plan. These activities happen independently of the other elements and this makes it difficult to thread the talent into the fabric of the organization.

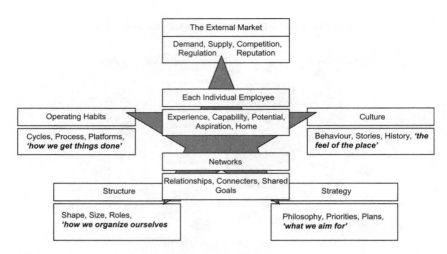

The constituents of talent ecology

The impact of the external market

From a talent perspective, what happens outside the organization is as important as what happens in it. It will pull and push your talent agenda, influencing the demand and supply of talent. Understanding the ebb and flow of your labour market and how this will impact your business is key. At a macro level this involves looking closely at education and employment patterns in your locations and in your sector. In addition:

• Pay close attention to competitor activity. Who are they hiring and where from? Who is leaving and where are they going to?

• Work with search firms to understand these dynamics and create market maps of those organizations or skills areas you aim to target.

• Be conscious of how your organization is perceived in the market. Do you have an employment brand that attracts the talent you need? More importantly, is your brand promise realistic? (It is worth repeating the wisdom of Andrew Mayo writing in his book *Human Value of the Enterprise* where he reminds us that 'brand' is Norse for 'promise'.)

The pivotal link with strategy

One common omission is the link to the business strategy. A quarter of organizations surveyed in a study by Cranfield School of Management and

Capital Consulting in 2007 admitted that their talent activities were not linked with the business strategy. As we have seen in Chapter 4, this is essential for planning the mix of skills, the volume and location of talent across the whole workforce. The strategic philosophy of the organization is also a vital consideration. This is rarely articulated in printed reports but relates to the implicit beliefs, assumptions and values at play. These are the priorities that the board and executive team talk about and often relate to the *intention* rather than the current reality of the organization. This type of intention is an ethereal concept and it is unlikely to have filtered far beyond the most senior managers. This said, being clear about the organization's intention, the future and will of its leadership team is necessary to shape the character of your talent activity. This character helps articulate the purpose of the talent activity, answering the questions 'why we are doing this' and 'what will be different as a result of this?' It is unfortunately still common for organizations to see the talent activity as an end in itself.

Talent – a valuable Trojan horse

Increasingly there are those organizations that intuitively see the link between the two strategies (business and talent) and shape their talent strategy as a delivery vehicle for the business strategy. Much like the famous Trojan horse, the organization should grasp the opportunity of using talent to drive the strategic business agenda. A number of companies now use the talent agenda as a change tool – a way of grounding their intentions and making them explicit. The Tata Corporation is one such company.

Established in the late nineteenth century, Tata is now India's largest private company by market capitalization with operations including steel, energy, car manufacturing and hotels. Philanthropy has long been an important part of this family-run company's activities and this is now evident in the importance they place on corporate social responsibility (CSR). Interestingly, their talent strategy is indistinguishable from their business and CSR strategies. As Adent Nadkarni, Tata's VP Corporate Social Responsibility explains, each is completely interdependent on the other. He talks about the intention of their business to 'create sustainable value' driven by leaders who work to demonstrate their capacity in three ways. First, by 'transcending' a given situation, recognizing that qualitative change is often the next step after incremental and quantitative change. Second, by being able to keep in balance many different factors and concerns; and third, by being able to get people to change their 'mindset'.

This interdependency of value, sustainability and leadership runs through the selection and development of managers. It is also evident in the ambition of the Chairman R.N. Tata who sees this integrated perspective as the distinguishing feature of Tata leaders. For Tata, the message for CEOs is that they need to adopt an integrated approach – they need to be profit oriented, cost effective and quality conscious, as well as good corporate citizens.

Talent loves talented company

The key point is to get underneath the business plan and articulate the *purpose* behind it. Often, as in the case of Tata, this is more than simply the desire to grow or to be more efficient. It should distil the essence of the organization into the simple difference it aims to make. Once this is articulated it needs to be designed into the infrastructure of the organization. How many companies could summarize it as succinctly as Google? Their '10 Reasons Why People Work With Us' is a people proposition that articulates how the business's ambition will come to life (see www. google.co.uk/support/jobs):

1. Lend a helping hand. With millions of visitors every month, Google has become an essential part of every day life, connecting people with the information they need to live great lives.
2. Life is beautiful. Being a part of something that matters and working on products in which you can believe is remarkably fulfilling.
3. Appreciation is the best motivation, so we've created a fun and inspiring workspace you'll be glad to be part of, including on-site doctor and dentist, massage and yoga; professional development opportunities; on site day care; shoreline running trails; and plenty of snacks to get you through the day.

4. Work and play are not mutually exclusive. It is possible to code and pass the puck at the same time.

5. We love our employees, and we want them to know it. Google offers a variety of benefits, including a choice of medical programs, company matched stock options, maternity and paternity leave and much more.

6. Innovation is our bloodline. Even the best technology can be improved. We see endless opportunity to create even more relevant, more useful, and faster products for our users. Google is the technology leader in organizing the world's information.

7. Good company everywhere you look. Googlers range from former neurosurgeons, CEOs, and US puzzle champions to alligator wrestlers and former Marines. No matter what their background, Googlers make for interesting cube mates.

8. Uniting the world, one user at a time. People in every country and every language use our products. As such we think, act and work globally – just our little contribution to making the world a better place.

9. Boldly go where no one has gone before. There are hundreds of challenges yet to solve. Your creative ideas matter here and are worth exploring. You'll have the opportunity to develop innovative new products that millions of people will find useful.

10. There is such a thing as a free lunch after all. In fact we have them every day – healthy, yummy and made with love.

Look beyond the constituent parts of the proposition, the West Coast optimism and the Star Trek reference and the purpose, philosophy and ambition are palpable. In talent terms they've done their homework. They clearly understand the demography of their internal (and external) labour markets and take care to understand their people, drawing out the clear relationship between the work they do and the wider, societal difference they can make. They also play to the fact that 'talent loves talented company' by emphasizing the quality and diversity of their workforce.

Great employers clearly understand the demography and diversity of their labour markets and take care to understand their people, valuing the clear relationship between the work they do and the difference they make. These employers also recognize that 'talent loves talented company' and emphasizes the quality and diversity of their workforce.

The forgotten role of structure

We live with so much change these days that we can be forgiven for thinking that organizational structure is all about the structure chart and the movements on it. This is particularly true when it comes to conventional talent management practices that are dominated by The Succession Plan, which looks like a structure chart. Adopting a *Talent Ecology* mindset provides a different perspective on structure, one that looks at how an operating model might generate talent, how roles can be adapted to retain talented individuals or how a hierarchy may now be frustrating the progression of talent. The novel aspect of this is that structural decisions should be made with talent in mind. This is different to the conventional view that the structure is omniscient, sitting above the character and needs of the individuals who live in it.

Of course, an organization's structure is simply the way it organizes itself to deliver its strategy. But boy has it got complicated: with Hay points, job evaluation, federations, matrices, divisions and networks. Whatever the model employed the job of the structure is to make activity efficient by giving people the space (roles) to apply their skills effectively. It is rare that we think about the adaptive potential of our structures from a talent perspective. We turn to re-structures when cost savings are required without ever asking how we could use the structure to attract, retain or mobilize talent better.

The idea of a company's structure following the dynamics of talent (rather than the other way around) came to prominence in Silicon Valley at the start of the dot.com era. One of the ideas that came along with this and has lasted longer than the office table football is the notion of structures designed to foster social capital. This was driven by the attention people started to give to the power of social networking as a work concept and as an on-line product. These early internet start-ups were simple forms of organization based around the energy and expertise of like minded individuals. Their early forms of organization were very much 'all hands to the pump affairs' with flat, networked forms of organization. Those that went on to survive the down-turn, have grown in complexity and adopted many of the organizational forms that we recognize in today's multi-nationals: operating divisions, functional back offices and group administrations.

Alongside these more conventional structures however they have carried through elements of work organization that are essential for knowledge-based product development and, from a talent perspective the attraction and engagement of knowledge workers.

The novelty of the propositions being worked on by these companies was (and is) dependent on multi-disciplinary perspectives. Search engine companies, for example, require mathematical, programming, analytics, engineering, telecommunications, marketing, customer experience and sales skills. They also require these skills to be mobilized quickly and applied to increasingly complex problems. These companies and those of a similar generation have learned that the way they organize provides a competitive edge in both the business and labour markets. Structures in these companies are driven to foster collaboration and innovation. There are fewer organization levels, smaller spans of control and work is driven more programmatically through inter-disciplinary projects. Formal organizational space and investment is also given to experiment and 'skunk work' type teams are encouraged. Companies such as Apple and Pixar also reach out into the families of employees, involving them in product prototyping or simply acknowledging the role they play in supporting their loved ones. Each of these structural forms is designed to strengthen the work between individuals, the aim being that the whole will become more than the sum of its parts. They are organizing for social capital knowing that this creates a dual talent benefit: more value from the talent they've got and a stronger employment brand for the talent they've yet to recruit.

The pithiest definition of social capital comes from Professor Nan Lin (Duke 2007) as an '*Investment in social relations with expected returns in the marketplace*'. We believe that the notion of social capital is relevant to the idea of *Talent Ecology* since it helps define the value that can be generated in the systems connecting individuals. From this perspective the idea of structure becomes more malleable, more orientated to where value can be generated as opposed to the static lines of the organization chart.

From structure chart to social capital
Social capital is the glue that holds the organization together; we believe that it offers an important insight into the way talent is actually realized by

the organization. In this respect social capital, 'the between employee factors' (teams, communities, networks, working groups) is an essential bedfellow to human capital 'the within employee factors' (skills, knowledge, experience and potential) which has dominated the talent agenda in recent times. The HR Blogger, Josh Letourneau comments via CruiterTalk.com:

> Ask yourself why there is so much focus on improving 'within-employee' factors (skills, competencies, etc.) when research is showing us that competitive advantage is more driven through the 'patterns of connections' (often called 'networks' or *'between-employee factors'*) than the mean level of organizational talent alone. According to Valdis Krebs, one of the foremost thinkers in the way of Social Network Analysis on the planet, *'Teams are not made of talent alone. It is how the talents of individual players intersect and interact that distinguishes a good team from a collection of good players ...'* Take a moment and ask yourself why organizations spend so much time focused on 'maintaining the formal structure [command-and-control] Org Chart' when they so rarely reflect how the day-to-day work gets done? Why is there such little focus on self-forming (in many cases) social networks when it is apparent 'how much information and knowledge flows through them and how little through official hierarchical and matrix structures'?

the new competitive edge in business is the organization's ability to appreciate context. This is the value created from the analysis, interpretation and insight of content and then the ability to turn this into new products or services. This type of value chain happens across many networks in an organization and as any Distribution Director will tell you the quality of the end product is entirely dependent on the quality of the relationships that created it.

HR blogger, Jon Ingham acknowledges this development but pragmatically points to how conventional and static the structures of today's organizations are, even those in Silicon Valley. We share his conclusion that although organizations have yet to catch up with this phenomenon, social capital is not dependent on flat or networked structures (although research shows that these certainly help). Social capital is generated by relationships and the key here is to invest in these relationships whether or not the structure has adapted to reflect them.

We believe that these connected relationships are becoming increasingly relevant to the talent agenda. As Valdis Krebs points out the new competitive edge in business is the organization's ability to appreciate context. This is the value created from the analysis, interpretation and insight of content and then the ability to turn this into new products or services. This type of value chain happens across many networks in an organization and as any Distribution Director will tell you the quality of the end product is entirely dependent on the quality of the relationships that created it. Being able to create and maintain these networked relationships is becoming a vital leadership skill in today's organization.

The importance of networks

The breadth of an individual's network is a good indicator of talent and future leadership potential. This is because it demonstrates an ability to access a range of resources and an ability to maintain relationships. Krebs urges the HR community to adopt a new mantra, 'hire and wire':

> In today's knowledge organization, the goal expands to 'hire-and-wire' − to hire the best people with the best network and integrate them into the value chain so that their combined human and social capital provide excellent returns.

The key to this is of course is that the individual can distinguish how to deploy this network in a way that is relevant to the project and team. Nevertheless, there is a growing evidence base to suggest that individuals with high social capital (Valdis Krebs, Working in the Connected World: Social Capital –The KillerApp for HR in the 21st Century, *IHRIM Journal* June 2000).

There are several advantages for talented people of having a great network, notably they:

- find better jobs more quickly;
- are more likely to be promoted early;
- close deals faster;
- receive larger bonuses;
- enhance the performance of their teams;
- help their teams reach their goals more rapidly;
- perform better as project managers;
- help their teams generate more creative solutions;

- increase output from their R&D teams;
- coordinate projects more effectively;
- learn more about the firm's environment and marketplace;
- receive higher performance evaluations.

Great networks rely on the qualities of what Malcolm Gladwell calls the Maven and the Connector. The 'Maven' being someone with deep expertise or opinion on a range of subjects and who enthusiastically shares this, while the 'Connector' has a driving interest in the experiences and passions of others and is able to find (or make) common ground between people. Although archetypes, these characters provide important insight into how talented people make connections and how creating social capital could be taught.

The nature of talented teams

This perspective on connectivity also gives us another way of looking at the role the team plays in an organization's Talent Ecology. Conventional ideas on talent tend to focus on the A-player, the star performer and neglect the importance of their interaction with colleagues. This infatuation with the talented individual has also neglected the idea of Talented Teams. These are the teams who consistently excel but without any star players. Their performance depends on the way they play to their strengths as a unit and in particular, how leaders emerge to galvanize this.

This insight has been popular in sport for some time. A feature about the 'Maryland Terps' (The University of Maryland's men's soccer team) in *Business Week* (August 2006) brings this to life. After six straight ACCA tournament showings, the Terps lost all of their star players to rivals in the late 1990s. By 2000 the team's performance plummeted to the bottom of the ACC league. Despite new hires and selecting his strongest players as co-captains, Coach Cirovski continued to watch performance decline. In desperation the coach turned to his brother, Vancho a HRD to provide ideas on improving their performance. Vancho's recommendation was to take a social X-Ray of the team and study how the network of relationships within the team worked. This involved analysing the pattern and quality of interactions between players, paying particular attention to how decisions were made. Vancho's findings dramatically altered the coach's view of leadership within the team. They discovered that by far the most influential player was a quiet sophomore, in skill terms more of a 'promising rather than sought after recruit'. He was the person each member of the team routinely engaged with, he moved between the team sharing news and connecting members with each other. The analysis showed that although this individual lacked maturity and obvious presence, the other team members routinely looked to him for direction. This insight drove Cirovski to make the quiet sophomore captain and to work on strengthening relationships across the team. Team members moved back onto campus, shared dorms and regularly socialized together. In terms of new hires Coach Cirovski started to look beyond the immediate star player and hired instead for personality, looking carefully for those players who could fit the chemistry of the team that was being created and resisting hiring at all if these could not be found.

This story, as you would hope, ends in success: the Terps went on to reach the National Championship. The postscript however was how highly sought after each of the players became, so much so that they were poached and the cycle started over again. The takeaway point here is that by building a talented team Cirovski was able to strengthen the capability of previously average individuals.

Adopting new habits

The value of the ties within the team compared to the value of a single star performer is also illustrated in articles on the New York Yankees (*New York Times* 2005) and the British Olympic Cycling team (*The Times*, March 2008). In each case the operating habits of the team proved to be a differentiating factor in how individuals were able to fulfil their potential. Interestingly, *The Times* article was written before the team's performance at the Beijing Olympics. In it David Brailsford, the team's Performance Director described the differences he had made to how the team was organized and how this was improving performance. Brailsford's work with the team can be generalized to reveal the habits that build a talented team.

- **Transfer natural ability between environments:** Rebecca Romero was a rowing world champion before joining the squad and both Victoria

Pendleton and Chris Hoy swapped from their favoured events into new disciplines.

• **Use the most innovative tools available:** to Brailsford the backroom team is as important as the athletes on the track. The team employed groundbreaking scientific techniques in every element of their preparation. From the design of the bikes, to the fabric in their suits and through to the athlete's nutrition.

• **Nurture the team dynamic and prepare the next generation:** the entire squad (including the juniors) were based together in Manchester. They trained together and socialized together. The more experienced athletes mentored their junior counterparts.

• **Turn the competition outwards:** each of the elite athletes has personal coaches and unusually for a squad at this level their coaches collaborated. This was unusual as the highly personal coach/athlete relationship can become insular viewing peers as competition. The cycling coaches became a team, sharing techniques and working on ways to beat their shared competition.

• **Set individual, incremental goals:** Brailsford was able to raise the performance of the whole team by giving each member highly personalized performance goals. Rather than a general focus on medals, these were grounded and tangible. Targets were focused on personal improvements in time and technique. These were routinely increased.

The British Cycling team left Beijing with fourteen medals, eight of them gold.

How culture can make or break a talent strategy

Culture is notoriously difficult to define and yet we all know it when we experience it. It's the culture that attracts people to organizations and is most often the reason they leave. We experience it directly through predominating behaviours and indirectly through the working processes, the 'way we do things around here'. It's an all-encompassing notion which drives the dynamic of the whole Talent Ecology. While recognizing that cultures will be as diverse as the organizations they are shaped into, we do believe that there are common features that attract and mobilize talent.

Digging big holes

A story from an energy company illustrates the reality of how a culture influences the attraction and development of talent. This large global group operates across each element of the energy supply chain: from petrol station forecourts through to production, exploration and renewables. Its business strategy had been to strengthen the efficiency of this chain and reduce operating cost. Its strategy for talent followed this and focused on creating enterprise-wide leaders who were rotated through different business models and markets. A succession pool of the top 200 high potentials was established and career paths across each of the different businesses were meticulously planned from the Group's Head Office. So far, so good, this begins to sound like a case study in good talent management practice. Until that is, we asked the question 'what do you have to do to get promoted around here?' The answer that came back on more than one occasion was: 'you dig big holes'. And, as if to really underline the route to the CEO's office, 'you dig the biggest holes'. Their evidence for this view was based on:

- The career histories of the most recent executive hires – the last two country MD hires were longstanding exploration veterans.
- The images used to illustrate the in house magazine and the recruitment literature and web site – lots of men with hard hats.
- CEO statements highlighting Upstream (exploration and production) as the 'growth' area and Downstream (refining and marketing) as the 'efficiency' area.

These important cultural signals combined to communicate an 'Upstream sexy, Downstream not' view in the pockets of the workforce. Our contacts told us of how culturally this suggested that career progress signified movement to out of the way places, macho environments and heavy machinery. This perception influenced many career decisions irrespective of the HR processes at play and while it certainly played to the strengths of some it probably diminished the supply of capability available to the organization overall. It also played against the best endeavours of the Group's HR team as they struggled to give their processes traction.

This example illustrates the pervasive effects of culture and provides a glimpse of the real character of the energy firm's Talent Ecology. In this case the talent strategy and process were fit for business purpose but the history of the place held it back; suggesting that the War for Talent had to be fought on multiple fronts:

- In the external labour market, telling stories of different career journeys and building an employment brand that attracts a diverse range of applicants.
- Making internal opportunities more transparent through on-line job boards advertizing vacancies all the way up to executive level.
- Updating the profile and competencies of key roles to reflect the desire to develop enterprise leaders.
- Reviewing promotion decisions. Are the decision makers mixed and able to offer a balanced view of 'what good looks like?'
- Employing a champion strategy, where senior leader communications are planned to reflect the messages of the talent strategy.

This final point is as ever a showstopper for every talent strategy to be effective. As Doug Ready and Jay Conger point out ('Make Your Company a Talent Factory' by Douglas A. Ready and Jay Conger, HBR, June 2007):

> Passion must start at the top and infuse the culture ; otherwise, talent management processes can easily deteriorate into bureaucratic routines.

The key issue here is that the messages the workforce received about their organization's beliefs on talent were at odds with each other. It is our experience that this lack of coherence runs across many organizations. There appears to be a belief that talent activity is such only when it is labelled talent. Ironically, the rise of the internal talent department has probably strengthened this belief. With companies falling into the trap of thinking it's the Chief Talent Officer's job to sort the talent problem. The siloed nature of the HR function

Sadly, too many companies appear to us to have got bogged down by the bureaucracy of Talent Management.

can also make it difficult to appreciate the levers for talent across the whole people agenda. Our view is that the talent agenda is so critical to the success of the organization that it needs to heavily influence the people strategy and culture. This means thinking through how a talent strategy can be delivered through the harder aspects of HR, performance, reward and employee relations. The risks of not joining these agendas are described below.

The revenge of the bell curve

A large telecommunication company had recently revamped its talent plans, introducing a new set of leadership competencies and recruiting brand. The drive for this refresh came from a need to recruit more future leaders and retain those already in post. The company was known in the market for developing good people and competitors were actively poaching talented individuals at all levels.

A change in market conditions prompted the CEO of this organization to embark on a mission to improve company performance through the introduction of the performance bell curve. Bell curves are based on relative, peer performance inside a team. This means that everyone would be judged against each other and a 0–5 rating applied accordingly (0 = poor performance, 5 = exceptional). The CEO insisted that all ratings achieved a formal percentage distribution of: 5, 15, 60, 15, 5 across the five point rating scale. This was applied without exception to every team irrespective of the team's operating conditions or achievement.

In performance terms, the bell curve is a well known tool to drive improved distribution of ratings and raise performance standards. In talent terms however, this tool can drive a number of unintended side effects. The firm's specialist functions – where there was highest demand in the external labour market and on whom the company depended – began to experience retention problems with a number of talented individuals. In exit interviews the leavers pointed to the perceived unfairness of the performance approach in general, the highest rated told of how their compensation had not been altered to reflect it and those rated as 'meeting their objectives' objected to the label since they did not feel it reflected their true contribution. This retention issue continues to be a problem and is beginning to impact on the firm's employment brand.

The issue here again is not the use of the bell curve itself (although arguably it is an approach that has had its day) but more about the incongruity of the messages. The firm's espoused talent strategy is meritocratic and focused on future opportunity. The performance philosophy means that you are only as good as your last rating and only the top 5% of performers in a given performance period come to the attention of senior leaders. This approach also destroys the social capital that could generate more talent. Peers compete with each other and there is very little room for collaboration, challenge or experimentation. These three characteristics are key to creating value and vital to those who create it.

Cultures that attract talent

Internet sites, such as 'Glassdoor.com', 'JobBeehive.com' and 'RateMyPlacement.co.uk' paint a candid picture of today's office culture. Here, current as well as ex-employees comment on aspects of their experience, from the salary to the socials. The sites attract a generation Y demographic who are certainly not afraid to hold back on their reviews. These reviews reflect the context of the companies they work for and reviewers rate their employers on everything from location, technology, management, learning and respect. They also provide advice to senior managers and rate the CEO. In most cases the reviews are relatively balanced and reasonable.

These sites highlight several points made in our research and elsewhere – that there does appear to be a common, cross generational need for:

1. **Work that is meaningful** – this means different things to every individual but we share a need to know that our effort makes a difference.
2. **Leaders we respect and trust (and who respect and trust us in return)** – talented people actively seek out mentors and role models, however the relationship needs to be reciprocated.
3. **Colleagues we can learn from** – talent loves company, all opportunities for collaboration are welcomed.
4. **Fair recognition and reward** – we are aware of our market value and believe this should be reflected in our pay packet. We need regular recognition, 'thank you' is enough.

5. **Opportunities to progress and/or keep learning** – we need to know that there are opportunities to progress, even if we aren't ready yet. When we reach a ceiling we want to know how to get better at what we do.

6. **Work-life balance** – we know that this will change over our careers but would like to be able to dial up and down as needed. Needing more time for life doesn't mean that we are less committed to our work.

7. **Being able to be ourselves** – we like to be treated as individuals and accepted for our quirks and passions. We are reassured when colleagues who are different to us are accorded the same respect.

8. **Being involved in decisions that affect us** – we have a view on how things could be better and we'd like to share this. We'll have to make the changes work so it's important we feel we've contributed to the goal.

9. **Being part of an organization that is respected** – our reputation goes with your reputation and we like to feel proud of where we work (or at least not embarrassed).

We asked our survey participants to comment on what would most influence their desire to work with an employer. This participant group had a strong Generation X bias and identified the following responses (see table below).

Which of these items would most influence your desire to work with an employer? (Participants rated the following items on a scale from 1 to 5, where 1 is the least influential and 5 the most.)

Factors influencing the appeal of a potential employer

	1	2	3	4	5	Avg
Undertake stimulating work	0%	0%	6%	28%	66%	4.6
An inspiring line manager	2%	3%	14%	43%	38%	4.1
A good corporate reputation and values	1%	5%	26%	25%	43%	4.0
Reward and benefits	–	8%	33%	39%	20%	3.7
Coaching and development	1%	11%	28%	35%	25%	3.7
Working with friendly co-workers	2%	11%	40%	32%	15%	3.5

Continued

	1	2	3	4	5	Avg
A clear career path	13%	23%	29%	21%	14%	3.0
Easy commute	11%	25%	38%	18%	8%	2.9
An attractive consumer brand	11%	34%	29%	21%	5%	2.7
Attractive offices	25%	42%	25%	8%	–	2.2

The clear lead item was the opportunity to 'Undertake stimulating work' (65.7%) followed by a 'Good corporate reputation and values' (42%) and 'An inspiring line manager' (37.9%). We also wanted to find out more information about what people felt helped them develop and succeed in their work, so we asked the same group:

Which of the statements best describe an organization that helps talent to thrive? (Participants rated the following items on a scale from 1 to 5, where 1 is the least influential and 5 the most.)

	1	2	3	4	5	N/A
Not sure that the organization is important, it depends on the people	18%	37%	17%	15%	11%	2%
A common purpose	1%	6%	18%	49%	26%	0%
Financial incentives	3%	18%	36%	36%	6%	0%
Clear performance management	1%	6%	13%	40%	39%	1%
Inspiring line managers	0%	(N/A)	2%	23%	69%	5%
Openness to new ideas	0%	(N/A)	1%	18%	75%	5%
Social networking is encouraged	(N/A)	4%	23%	46%	26%	1%
Time for development	0%	0%	6%	39%	51%	3%
Regular job rotations	1%	5%	26%	39%	27%	2%
Diversity is welcomed	0%	2%	10%	33%	50%	4%
Executives are accessible	0%	1%	9%	33%	54%	3%
Regular contact with customers/clients	0%	3%	19%	39%	36%	3%

Developing the talent ecology

The idea that it's the whole of the organizational system that makes talent activity effective is not new. It is however, often ignored. Leaders retrench to tangible, manageable activities that are easily measured. Or, with limited investment pots they opt for one or two activities that promise an easy return on investment.

We believe that given the potential benefits, working on your Talent Ecology requires very modest financial investment; remember the levers you need to work on already exist, it's about being able to deploy them in the round. It is also possible and important to set targets and measure progress. The most important macro measure is the progress your organization is able to make towards its strategic goals. At a more detailed level, measurement around the areas that drive this for example:

- an improved cost income ratio;
- faster speed to market;
- higher customer satisfaction and retention;
- a wider membership base;
- increased sales and share of wallet.

All are indicators that talent is growing in your organization. Get underneath the success stories and ask how it happened. Was it driven by:

- a new hire to the organization?
- the skill of the local leader?
- an improvement in front-line skills?
- the performance of a particular team?

Share these stories and consider the implications for disseminating the people and the practice across the organization. Goals around other people activities should complement rather than drive this. Recruitment, Turnover, Performance, Reward distribution, Learning and Engagement are important. How employees experience these operating habits should also be captured.

Aiming for a 'fly wheel' effect

In the seminal book *Good to Great*, writer Jim Collins demonstrated how companies were able to make the transition to excellence. His research demonstrated the vital interplay of leadership, culture and talent – namely, getting the right people on the bus. He also noticed that companies succeeded because of coherence and consistency in these areas.

Collins defined coherence 'as the magnifying effect of one factor on another'. We believe that this is exactly how to look at the balance of your Talent Ecology. The famous Harvard case study on GE's talent practices, 'How to Build a Talent Factory', also underlines this and the need to keep working on getting better at developing your organization to develop people's potential.

Jack Welch famously implemented the 9 Box matrix and founded Crotonville, but he also acknowledged that his contribution was strengthening a culture of talent which had started with Thomas Edison. We would argue that at GE it was not the tools that mattered, rather it was the tradition and time (Welch allocated three days a week!) given to developing the organization's capacity to develop potential. And, that this capacity was entirely integrated into their business and their expectation of leaders. At GE talent simply became 'the way we do things around here' featuring in all aspects of their operating system.

GE had created a Talent 'Fly Wheel', taken small, incremental steps that gradually built momentum until each piece of the system reinforces the other parts of the system, forming an integrated whole that is more powerful than the sum of the parts.

Leadership reflections

Ultimately, an effective Talent Ecology is also about how you and your fellow leaders choose to lead your organization. Take care not to get bogged down by the bureaucracy of talent processes like succession planning – they have their place but are simply tools to help you 'Hire and Wire' talent into your organization. The following points are places to start influencing the talent ecology and moving that flywheel.

1.   How well do you understand the capability of your existing work-force and the extent to which it will meet the needs of your organization into the future?

2.   Do you understand which type of skills you will need and where you will get them from? Is it worth getting to know your competitor's people and keeping close to target recruits so that they understand your business when you are ready to recruit them?

3.   Are you clear about why people would work for you (and your organization)? Are you prepared to adapt if your target audience needs something else?

4.   Is your employment brand explicit and compelling? Are you making sure that your external and internal communications reflect this brand?

5.   Are you inclusive in your approach to talent? Do you and your leaders accept that the engagement of your whole workforce is vital for your business's performance?

6.   Do you differentiate your workforce by their capacity to drive value? Remember that leaders of the future will not look like leaders today. Increased diversity will provide a broad, flexible portfolio of talent.

7.   Would it be useful to upgrade your HR infrastructure and focus on two things: the quality of the employee experience and providing line managers with the tools and the time to develop potential?

8.   Do you review your structure and the roles within it regularly? Can you anticipate vacancies and secondments and make these accessible through internal job boards?

9.   Are you connecting with people, recognizing networks and networkers? Do you encourage communities of shared interest?

10.   Are you encouraging leadership irrespective of grade? Do you recognize and reward the team-players, teachers and innovators? Let these internal leaders design and deliver employee education programmes.

In this chapter we highlighted the need for leaders to hire, wire and develop their organization's talent; it's now time to understand how the workplace can encourage people to bring all of their talents to work. This matters, because people who are realizing their potential and stretching their abilities are more likely to achieve more for themselves and their employers.

Chapter 6

Getting Personal: The Workforce of One

There are two dominant organizational metaphors of man – man as machine, where people are interchangeable parts and will perform equally well across a range of circumstances; and homo economicus, man as a rational, economic maximizer who will behave in a rational manner and make choices which maximize the results of his labour. These metaphors dominated our early thinking on how organizations were structured, how jobs were assigned, and how performance was encouraged through reward and punishment. They failed to capture the complexity of individuals, by assuming everyone was the same when in fact they were very different, and by overestimating rational behaviour and underestimating the part played by our will and our emotions. Yet to move from the machine and the economic metaphor is to create a more complex world, where factors such as emotions and hopes are intangible and inordinately complex and the interdependencies understood only over time, and where people are seen as individuals rather than 'the workforce'.

Lynda Gratton, *Living Strategy* (FT Prentice Hall, page 75)

Bringing your talents to work

It is time to talk about talented organizations and how the workplace can encourage people to bring all of their talents to work. This means, as far as possible, that people are not only realizing their potential but also stretching their abilities in new, enjoyable and fulfilling directions. Our research tells us that there are several emerging issues:

- The need for organizations to segment their workforce and understand the priorities, character, strengths and weaknesses of different groups of employees.
- The importance of their moving beyond groups and aggregation to personalize each individual's contract of employment (informally as well as formally).
- The value of recognizing these psychological contracts to each employee – this means understanding issues of behaviour, personality and self-awareness, notably including emotional intelligence.

Above all, talented organizations recognize that everyone is in the talent team: top executives, people management professionals, each individual leader or manager, and each employee. It recognizes that the best employees increasingly want work to be more meaningful – stimulating, worthwhile and responsible. For leaders this means answering a vital question: 'how can you make work more personal for your team?'

Life just got personal – the trend to mass customization

The rise of Web 2.0 is accelerating our ability to interact and shape our experiences on line. It reflects a growing interest in user generated and participatory content originally made popular through sites like You Tube and Second Life. This growing appetite for creative experiences has been recognized by marketers and we are now more able to customize our consumption in almost every area of our lives. We can create personal radio stations, create our own news filters, make our own ring tones and create our personal supermarket aisle. Google remembers our searches and Amazon remembers our purchases. Both are able to recommend next steps based on our personal preferences.

Being able to personalize who we are and how we live is now the 'new normal' and yet when we look at work the closest we can get to this is the way we decorate our desks.

This trend has also moved into tangible products; you can design your own trainers at Nike.com, add stripes (or checks) to your Mini car and add your child's photo to your credit card. In the high street we can customize our coffee mixing several options across volume, roast, bean, strength, flavouring and fat, (at the last count). We can still remember a time when our only options were with milk or sugar.

This trend towards mass customization has been driven by two important developments: a greater capacity to understand consumer's behaviour, powered by new technologies and more sophisticated (and lower cost) methods of production. This has led to businesses postponing the challenge of differentiating a product for a specific customer until the last possible opportunity.

Offering a customized proposition is perceived as an important way of adding value to the consumption experience. Marketers are able to do this by understanding the demographic profile and behaviour of different customer groups. How often you log on to a particular site, the number of mobile minutes you use (or don't use), the books you prefer to browse, the expenditure on your current account. Patterns of activity can be predicted and the offer, or proposition, can be shaped according to what you might do next.

This ability to customize our consumption is a significant development in our social lives. It works across the range of our most fundamental needs. We can self actualize; create new identities as avatars, becoming better than it's possible to be in real life. Or we can use it to make life simpler, filtering out the noise of other choices and focus on the familiar and convenient.

Being able to personalize who we are and how we live is now the 'new normal' and yet when we look at work, the closest we can get to this is the way we decorate our desks.

We believe the talent agenda is intimately connected with the trend towards mass customization. We all have a need to be recognized for who we are as individuals. It influences where we want to work as well as how we work. It greatly influences how we come to trust and connect with our manager and the wider organization. Most importantly, being recognized for who we are is the key to unlocking discretionary potential.

The rise of the employer brand

One of the first shots to be fired in the War for Talent was the idea of the employer (or employment) brand. In the late 1990s this focused on companies strengthening their presence in the labour market and chiefly consisted of improving their communications to prospective recruits. Mainly, this involved finding appealing images for the target audience (usually graduates) and adding the company's mission statement to the new website.

In time this has grown more sophisticated and moved beyond the on-line brochure. Far sighted companies have started to get to grips with understanding the emotional connection of their brands and how it influences people's choices on whether to stay or to leave. This requires substantial research into people's current perceptions of the organization, how it works and its reputation. The most insightful studies also dig down into the level of personal or group engagement and focus in on the reality of day to day life in the organization. Sadly, however, this is rare and the majority of branding work still appears to think about the brand as a strictly recruitment-led PR tool.

Of course every employer has a brand whether it is communicated consciously or unconsciously and this will shape the psychological contract. A study by the Corporate Research Forum (CRF, The Employer Brand and Employee Engagement 2005) summarized four elements of an effective employer brand:

- Trust in the employer-employee relationship.
- Inspiration for people to commit to the organization beyond basic expectations.
- Differentiation in clarifying why and how the employer brand is different and better than others.
- Brand segmentation which makes the brand adaptable to different needs, expectations, audiences, job markets, operating conditions etc.

This last point on segmentation is significant since it is an important means of reaching the individual inside the complex, changing workforce.

The value of segmentation
Segmentation can be defined as the process of dividing a market according to similarities that exist between various subgroups within that market. These similarities may be common attributes or perspectives, or shared

needs and desires. In fact, there are four basic market segmentation strategies: behaviour segmentation, demographic segmentation, geographic segmentation, and physiographic segmentation. Market segmentation results from the simple view that all potential users of a product are not alike, they differ, and as a result the same general qualities will not appeal to everyone. Because of this, it then becomes essential to develop different marketing tactics designed to connect with different potential users, so that the entire market for a particular product is covered.

The idea is that leaders need to be able to segment their workforce into specific groups so that they can play to the strengths of each set of individuals. This skilfully combines a need for information and analysis with a creative, people-centred approach.

A senior marketing colleague once remarked that he wanted to see 'all of our customers broken down by age and sex', what he meant was he wanted to better understand the customers: who they are and what they value. This enabled him to match products with customers, as well as informing his thinking about many other issues: from new product development to pricing and distribution. This is the challenge of segmentation. Many industries and businesses are improving their market segmentation, for example, by using psychographic profiling that divides customers into 'groups' according to personal needs, preferences and lifestyle.

The overriding priority is to help people: segmentation is a means to an end. It works best alongside an understanding of each individual, not instead of such an understanding. The goal is to understand and support people better, focusing your approach and resources more effectively to help the individual realize their potential.

There are several other important points to bear in mind when segmenting a workforce:

- Segmentation needs to be focused: the larger a segment is the greater the danger that it will lose value.
- The value of segmentation lies in highlighting differences and specific characteristics: this requires clarity and insight.
- Segmentation should be as simple as possible, by avoiding unnecessary complications and ensuring decisions and views are rational and clear.

- Segmentation needs certainty. It is tempting to jump to conclusions or make assumptions about segments based on one's own experience, background or prejudice. However, these can be mistaken and a key element in successful segmentation is analysis: understanding how something is and why it is that way.

Marketers often split consumers into dozens of groups. These are sometimes driven by postcode and/or by lifestyle choices. Thus we have for example, DINKYs (dual income, no kids), Duty Free Dads (prefer to spend their kids' inheritance on enjoying life now) and Digital Natives (sometimes referring to young Generation Y and Zs, the first generation not have to migrate to digital technology).

These are archetypes of course but segmentation is a technique that can be used in organizations to get us closer to thinking about people in a more personalized way.

Understanding memetics

Closely linked with the concept of segmentation is the idea of memetics. Memetics reveals how ideas spread through society, take hold and influence our everyday activities and decisions. The notion is that social, political and cultural ideas (known as memes) are copied between individuals and groups, and are then passed on again and again through a variety of means. If a meme is particularly good at making sure it is easily copied, can spread quickly and is durable, then it is more likely to exert an influence over the way that groups think and act.

The truth is that we naturally imitate others – it is one way that we learn. Our default programme is to copy others, and whenever we copy someone we are following a meme. Because this method is hardwired into us, it is understandable that we should continue using this mechanism in all aspects of our lives. Unappealing as it may seem, fashions, values, behaviours, language, religion, attitudes and beliefs are imitated and passed on through groups and down to subsequent generations.

Memes are powerful and are referred to as the cultural equivalent of genes, as they are transferred between individuals, spread through society and passed on to successive generations. There is another reason that they are equated to genes: memes are seen as critical to individuals' and groups' ability to survive and prosper in society, and to ensuring that subsequent generations are successful. This is why ideas, fashions and beliefs exert such powerful influences over us: if we accept them, we will belong to the 'in group' and are more likely to prosper; if we ignore them, we will be seen as an outsider and are likely to be ostracized and to fail.

It is easy to see why memes are so powerful: the rewards of belonging to a group (and the penalties of not belonging) are too great and compelling, and they are fundamental to the way people interact. The bonding, cohesiveness and strength that memes promote have all contributed to the survival and success of people and groups in society. Significantly, strong and durable groups can hold values that others would disagree with – even be appalled by. All that matters is the survival of the meme – the survival of values that the group holds.

Success often depends on our ability to challenge and change our own attitudes and perceptions, our methods of working and how we deal with others.

While there are undoubtedly positive aspects of memes, such as helping people and societies progress, it can be inherently difficult to recognize and change negative aspects of ourselves and our organizations. After all, a meme comes about because someone (or some group) wants to continue exerting power over others. It is not in the meme's interest to give up easily – its existence implies that it has a strong hold on people's behaviour and thinking and that it is not easily challenged.

However, progress and competitive advantage can rely on our ability to see things from another person's point of view (for example, when dealing with customers, colleagues and competitors in markets that have other beliefs, conventions, fashions, values etc.). Success can also rely on our ability to challenge and change our own attitudes and perceptions, our methods of working and how we deal with others.

By recognizing the power that our colleagues, other people, companies, groups and society have on us through the myriad of memes, we are better equipped, as individuals and as organizations, to evaluate issues accurately, to challenge conventions and current methods of working, to make effective decisions and to improve both our personal effectiveness and the success of our organizations.

So, how can you make memes work for you? The first point is to understand that we are more likely to help people we recognize as being like us in some way and, therefore, associate with – even if they are strangers. It is also valuable to me that individuals can invariably achieve more when they work together as a group and can clearly see and feel that they have something in common with each other. Therefore, it is vital to have a compelling vision and clear goals communicated in a meaningful way for each group of employees. Organizations with clearly understood goals and direction can harness the power of memetics for each specific group, countering the constraints of the past and bringing people together.

Segmenting talent

Talent management lends itself well to segmentation and memetics since it asks us to differentiate different types of talent and the value it provides to the organization. A way of doing this for the whole workforce has to be to look at key drivers of talent – like for example, performance and then to correlate the characteristics of those falling into key performance groups. We recommend always correlating at least two data sets e.g. performance and gender, performance and bonus, performance and age to start to highlight those groups that might merit further exploration.

Techniques for rating performance
Taking performance ratings as a good example, questions to ask include:

- Are there any noticeable differences by demographic (age, gender, ethnicity)?
- Does length of service play a role?
- What's the three-year trend on (for example) bonus pay?
- Who is being promoted most frequently?

You should pay particular attention to:

- The highest and lowest performers.

- The group where there have been significant changes in performance (high to low or low to high).
- Bonus awards – often the payment of bonus and performance rating don't coincide! This is especially the case in cultures where there is a forced distribution of ratings, managers play the rating game but use bonus as a real rating. Subject to the wider bonus environment, this is a good indicator of finding employees who are adding value.
- The 'Nine Box Matrix' offers a ready-made segmentation. The dilemma with using this is the frequency with which your talent strategy might expect people to move through the boxes. For example, once a 'high potential' is promoted, their performance level is likely to drop moving them to a different segment.

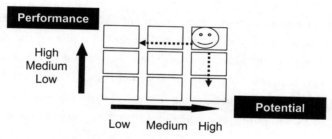

Typical performance/potential or nine box matrix

This analysis depends on the quality of employee data and also timing. We recommend using data that is consistent for a given time period, usually one year, while building profiles of key segments.

Using employee data

Employee data can be a headache, however don't aim for perfection. Use the data you do have to locate and sketch out key segments, then follow these up with face-to-face interviews and focus groups. This qualitative research is essential to really get to know the people who are typical of the segment you are creating. At this stage it can be a worthwhile investment to bring in expert market researchers. The aim of this research is to understand more about the influences on the segment, their beliefs and their behaviour. In consumer based marketing the research goal would be to find insights. These insights might point to an underpinning reason for a belief or a behaviour. This could be an unmet need, reaction to the attributes of a new product or the perceived benefits of a service.

In the instance of performance we might for example, want to learn more about:

- The characteristics of our highest performers, what they do to achieve results and their drivers for meaning and ongoing engagement.
- The characteristics of our lowest performers, what is not working, what do they need to get back on track.
- What the managers of these groups do – this may be an important group to segment.

This type of employee research is also important at different stages in the employee life-cycle. Consider studying reactions on joining the company and then again within twelve months (when engagement levels often drop). Look at what happens when people get promoted and when they leave. In this respect we recommend going beyond the simple exit survey and forming an alumni group, you may always want to persuade them to come back.

The groups moving through each of these stages will be transient, however over time you will be able to build up a typical picture of met and un-met needs across the employee experience.

Segmentation provides an important tool for building up a picture of a dynamic, heterogeneous workforce. Its real value however is in the insight it gives us in the development of products and services to target these needs.

Getting beneath the Employee Value Proposition

An Employee Value Proposition (EVP) refers to the reward, experience and opportunities an employee receives when working with a particular employer. This is wider than just contractual terms, it is the practical delivery of the Employment Brand.

We highlighted Google's 'Ten Reasons Why People Work With Us' in Chapter 6 and this is a good example of a generic Value Proposition. It clearly articulates what the firm expects from its people and what they will provide in return. Importantly, the proposition itself has been honed to reflect the needs and preferences of the people they aim to attract and retain.

Innocent (the drinks company) has also given this some thought using snapshots of employees with a hand written note on the things people like (all quotes reproduced with permission of Innocent). These are quirky and thoughtful like the people they employ. Their proposition is described as 'Life at Innocent'. This is separated into 'the important stuff' and 'the nice stuff'. The first section talks about money in a refreshingly transparent way:

> In a nutshell, our philosophy is that everyone should get something, but the people contribute the most get the most.

They go on to detail each element of pay, highlighting a 'nest egg' offering discounted shares to high performers and shares on your anniversary so that 'everyone gets a little skin in the game'. The 'nice stuff' really illustrates the investment the company makes in bringing their EVP to life. There are nature weekends, foundation scholarships – giving colleagues an extra week's holiday to go make a difference, clubs, an extra week's holiday for your wedding/civil partnership, childcare, yoga and breakfast. Our favourite is their ironic take on recognition; they cheerfully promote a monthly 'Lord or Lady of the Sash Award':

> Every month we all vote for the person that has been extra special, gone that bit further than they needed or just been really nice. They get a sash and a top hat/tiara and get to have tea made for them by minions.

Their quirkiness is serious, however, because, when you look at the profile of the people they want to hire, people who have 'the smarts', the ability to think round problems, deal with ambiguity and create new opportunities, these are the same people who this is aimed at.

The value of early segmentation work should help you shape your proposition to the groups you most want to target. Crucially, any EVP which looks good on the website must work as well inside the organization. It should also be sufficiently coherent to travel into customized propositions for each of your target segments. We recommend that like Innocent you are transparent about how you differentiate propositions between groups. Your Talent Strategy should spell out how value is driven, identified and recognized. For example, you might:

- Talk about the career development available for those demonstrating potential to move into bigger roles.
- Highlight holiday flexibility for long service.
- Support professional body qualifications and membership for specialists.
- Provide supported sabbatical to high performers reaching a significant life transition.

We also recommend that you make it easy to see how employees can move between different propositions.

Leadership reflections

We've mentioned earlier that the value of your proposition is only as good as the experience people have when it's landed. This is the toughest part of the employment brand equation and is entirely dependent on the commitment of your line mangers and the quality of your HR system.

- Line managers hold the key to understanding the personal drives of every employee. Invest time in showing them why it's important and how to do it.
- Consider how well your assessment and selection process reflects your target audience and the impression you are trying to make. We've both encountered firms extolling the values of 'agility, fairness and transparency', to discover that selection results can take weeks to be communicated with very little consideration given to what went well (or didn't).
- When things are personal, the smallest things matter. Welcoming people, celebrating birthdays and saying goodbye are all Brand touch points.

- We know that when things aren't working well, employees most often lose touch with the organization in their first year. Help them build a 'First 90 day' plan and ensure they have a properly supervised on-boarding. It's no longer just a question of being told the IT helpline and where the toilets are, even the most senior executives need introductions to key influencers and networks.

- How labour intensive is your performance appraisal cycle? It is our experience that people get caught up in writing forms, reviewing forms, waiting for ratings approval, calibration and finally feedback. Very little time is given to celebrate, feedback or discuss the setting of new objectives.

- How often do you use feedback as part of your development and engagement approach? Unfortunately feedback is a term used to dress up the delivery of bad news. It is essential to communicate *why* people may or may not have access to certain resources as well as reinforcing what's working well. The fact that you noticed matters.

- Reward is the backbone of everyone's employment proposition. Often the thing that matters most is not 'more' reward but 'fair' reward. Everyone needs to know how what they're making compares to their counterparts – and while we wouldn't recommend sharing personal details – we absolutely recommend being bold with your reward philosophy. It is also important to remember that different aspects of reward matter differently to different people (at different times). Pensions are critical to Boomers but less so to Generation Y. Generation X'ers may trade for more holiday. Flexible benefits schemes bring an important element of personal choice and control into the reward proposition.

- Good development requires dedicated investment. This is not just the formal programme but also the work shadowing experience or secondment. It is essential that employees take ownership for their learning agenda, however, we do believe that the organization also has a role to play in providing time for the learning to take place and guidance around the experience. We notice and recommend an increasing trend towards modularity in learning, allowing employees to create customized pathways which they are able to follow at their own time and at their own pace.

- Rotations are important for everyone not just the highest performers. They help disseminate new practices which revive the careers of employees who might have stagnated. Make it easy (and rewarding) for line managers to give their talent. Make it simple for employees to re-locate and provide support as they make this transition.

• Review how employees are able to customize their roles. It is important to be able to understand when people are able to take on additional responsibilities and when they need to step back. This is particularly important when retaining talented women and people from under-represented groups.

The next chapter explains how to make sure that leaders and their organizations are actively engaging with their employees.

Chapter 7

Engaging With Talent

It is often said that people don't leave their employer, they leave their boss. In other words, people need to be led so they are fully engaged with their work. In this chapter we discuss how leaders can best relate to their colleagues. How do you know them and what do they think? Above all, how can leaders make sure their people are engaged, even inspired, and enthusiastic about their work? What is often needed is an understanding of why engagement matters and what it can accomplish, as well as other practical measures.

Employee engagement: what it is and why it matters

The thinking behind employee engagement is simple. If people in organizations are actively engaged with their work – not simply motivated, but valuing what they are doing and striving to do it better at all times – then they will be more productive for the organization, as well as more fulfilled and likely to achieve personal career success.

The logic and evidence for this view is compelling: it works, and works well. The challenge, however, is to move from a situation where people might (or might not) be simply happy and motivated, to one where they are actively loyal, committed and engaged with their work. The first part of this toolkit explains how employee engagement works and why it is so significant, giving examples of firms that have developed and benefited from greater engagement. The second part provides practical techniques to help you generate greater employee engagement within your team.

Employee engagement can be divided into two types:

- Rational commitment – this is when a job meets an employee's financial, developmental or professional self-interest. It is most often associated with traditional approaches to motivation, and the view that an important part of a manager's job is to create a motivating environment.
- Emotional commitment – this goes further than traditional motivation, and arises when workers are not only satisfied and content in their work (i.e. motivated), but actively value, enjoy and believe in what they do. These 'true believers' are the employees who are most successful: they are of greatest value to the business and, consequently, tend to go furthest in their careers.

Research by the Corporate Leadership Council suggests that emotional commitment has four times the power to improve performance. They found that:

- 11% of workers demonstrate very high levels of both types of commitment.
- 13% demonstrate very little of either type of commitment.
- 76% are moderates: people who generally exhibit a strong commitment to one person or element of their job, but can take or leave the rest. Consequently, their intent to leave is variable. Also, according to researchers, this group neither shirks nor strives.

The thinking behind employee engagement is simple. If people are actively engaged with their work – not simply motivated but valuing what they are doing and striving to do it better at all times – then they will be more productive for the organization, as well as more fulfilled and likely to achieve personal career success.

These figures are likely to be broadly similar for all major corporations. The challenge, therefore, is to support and encourage as many moderates as possible to commit even further to their job, for the benefit of everyone.

The benefits of engagement

Some executives believe that issues of engagement, commitment and even motivation are pointless distractions – employees are paid to work, and money is all that matters. This old-fashioned view is not supported by research or evidence. People are complex, changeable, multi-talented individuals, and they are expensive. So, it makes sense to try to get the best out of every individual. Not only is this best for the business: it is more satisfying and worthwhile for everyone, including managers.

More than that, there is a great deal of proof that employees' engagement and commitment directly affects:

- productivity;
- satisfaction;
- retention.

Productivity is clearly important for the business, but being productive leads directly to a sense of achievement and personal fulfilment.

Satisfaction matters because people who are satisfied work better, harder and more effectively. It also enables businesses to attract and retain the best people.

Retention matters because it is expensive to recruit and train people, and an inability to retain people disrupts teamwork, customer service and productivity. This element can therefore make the whole process of employee engagement self-sustaining (as shown in the diagram below).

A virtuous, self-sustaining cycle resulting from employees who are engaged with their work.

What affects employee engagement?

The truth is that almost anything about an individual and their job can affect the way that people (complex beings as they are) engage with their work.

First, however, an important caveat: this chapter and, indeed, most of this book, starts from the premise that most people have choices, they choose their career and, at least initially, have some choice about the work they do. Clearly, there are many millions of people in the world who do not have this choice about their work, and while there are some useful insights in this book for them the concepts of talent, engagement and leadership as a whole are admittedly less relevant. For example, if you are an Ethiopian farmer struggling to avoid famine then your work and the issues you face have their own distinctive, demanding and highly challenging character.

For many other people there is a wide range of influences on their feelings of engagement at work, and each influence has a personal significance for them. This results from their personality, experiences and character. Some of the most significant possible influences are listed below – the crucial point is that these combine for different people in different ways, and at varying times. If you haven't done this before it might be personally useful and revealing to reflect on this list and consider what matters most to you, as well as *why* and *when* it matters. Perhaps mark each item out of 10. Also, is anything missing from this list for you?

Rewards
1. Compensation
2. Health benefits
3. Retirement benefits
4. Holiday

The Opportunity
5. Development opportunities
6. Opportunities for personal growth or benefit
7. Future career opportunities
8. The organization's rate of growth

9. Meritocracy
10. Organizational stability and security

The Organization
11. Customer reputation
12. Diversity
13. Empowerment
14. Environmentally responsible
15. Ethical

The Employer
16. Recognition

17. Interesting or appealing industry
18. Informal work environment
19. Strong market position
20. Product brand awareness
21. Product quality
22. Respect
23. Risk taking
24. Organization size
25. Socially responsible
26. Technology level is appealing

The Work

27. Business travel
28. Innovation
29. Job impact (content or the ability to make a difference)
30. Alignment between the job and your interests

31. Location
32. Recognition
33. Work–life balance

The People

34. Camaraderie and collegiality
35. Supportive
36. Interesting

37. Coworker quality
38. Manager quality
39. Opportunity to manage people
40. Reputation of senior leadership

Of all these items, there are two that stand out: pay and leadership. Pay is a complex subject but it is worth remembering a simple, fundamental fact that can often be overlooked as we develop ever more sophisticated organizations and structures, and it is this: there is a direct, permanent relationship between pay and effort. In fact, the two correlate extremely closely and pay affects behaviour, acting as an incentive. It is a source of constant surprise to me how often organizations expect their employees to do more or different things, yet they completely ignore the fact that the new or additional action has a price. Similarly, people seem to forget that their labour has a value to the organization: workers' expectations or demands for pay have both to be affordable and realistic, yet this is simply ignored. Also, it seems that from time to time both organizations and individuals believe they are unique (true) and that this means they are irreplaceable (untrue). So, if you are an employer, accept that your employees can go elsewhere at any time and act accordingly; and if you are an employee, accept that you can always be replaced by someone else. If everyone took this approach then, perhaps, organizations and people would work better together.

It is also worth remembering the fundamental economic truth that lies at the heart of capitalizm: one that is so fundamental it is invariably overlooked. *Profitability requires scarcity* and this is increasingly provided by the uniqueness of knowledge, skills and people. The more abundant the supply of a good or service, the lower its price will be. The more scarce the supply, the more likely the good or service is to generate a profit or a greater return. In the pharmaceuticals industry, for example, if there is a high demand for a product for which you have a patent and no alternative exists, the future is a lucrative one, even if the research and development costs have been substantial. Thus scarce and valuable knowledge can help deliver exceptional profits.

The issue of leadership is similarly complex. It is often said that people don't leave their organization, they leave their boss. For individual employees their leaders provide a guiding view of the future that influences their decisions, priorities and way of working. People generally like to do work that is meaningful or at least purposeful. Strong leadership provides and explains that purpose. In this way it helps to give individual fulfilment. This psychological element points to an important fact about leadership: the intangible and valuable contribution it makes to employees' commitment, engagement, productivity, creativity and success. Simply put, people work better and achieve more if they believe in what they are doing and have confidence in the direction they are going. Conversely, uncertainty or insecurity about the future breeds tension, lack of confidence and even cynicism, none of which are conducive to business success or personal achievement. Finally for individuals, effective leadership enables individuals to develop their personal potential and, invariably, to attain new skills. This then initiates a self-sustaining cycle of confidence, self-awareness and success.

As we shall see, pay and leadership (and the need for work to have meaning) are far from the only issues that matter and, indeed, what is important varies according to each individual employee. But few other issues are as ubiquitous or significant. They are 'table stakes' without which employees and organizations would suffer hugely.

Three-factor theory

How do you get people to work? What we mean is: how can leaders get their team members to be fully engaged, inspired and energized, looking for ways that they and the business can achieve more and go even further? There is a wide range of theories of motivation that attempt to answer this question and the best are based on practical observation and actual results. It is worth considering two approaches that are particularly interesting:

three factor theory, pioneered by Sirota Consulting, and the service-profit chain first highlighted by US retailer Sears.

Three-factor theory is based on the premise that workers have basic human needs that managers should address. Creating an environment in which these needs are met results not just in satisfied employees but enthusiastic employees.

During the period 1994 to 2003, US-based firm Sirota Consulting surveyed 237 organizations worldwide across a range of industries, providing more than two million responses.* No single sector was more than 14% of the total. Sirota's research suggests that there are three primary sets of goals for people at work (known as the 'three factor theory'): *equity, achievement* and *camaraderie*. It should be noted that the conclusions of this research are *nearly* universal, as they apply to 95% of employees.

These three goals characterize what the overwhelming majority of employees want – for most workers, no other goals are nearly as important. These goals have not changed over time (at least recent time) and they cut across demographic groups and cultures. In Sirota's view, establishing policies and practices in tune with these goals is the key to employee engagement.

The three-factor theory is based on the premise that workers have basic human needs that management can and should work to address. Creating an environment in which these needs are met results not just in satisfied employees but *enthusiastic* employees.

Equity

This means being treated justly in relation to the basic conditions of employment. These basic conditions are:

- **Physiological,** such as having a safe working environment or manageable workload.
- **Economic,** including such issues as pay, benefits and job security.

---

* For further details see *The Enthusiastic Employee: How Companies Profit by Giving Workers What They Want* by David Sirota, Louis A. Mischkind and Michael Irwin Meltzer, Wharton School Publishing, 2005.

- **Psychological** – being treated consistently, fairly, considerately and with respect.

Feelings of equity are influenced by a sense of *relative* treatment. For example, am I being treated fairly in relation to my peers and colleagues?

Achievement

This means: taking pride in one's accomplishments by doing things that matter and doing them well; receiving recognition for one's accomplishments, and taking pride in the team's accomplishments. Sirota Consulting's research suggests that this sense of achievement has six primary sources:

- *The intrinsic challenge* of the work and the extent to which an employee can apply their skills and abilities.
- *Acquiring new skills* and the opportunity to develop, take risks and expand personal horizons.
- *Ability to perform* – and possessing the resources, authority, information and support to do the job well.
- *Perceived importance of the job* – employees need to feel that their work has a purpose and value.
- *Recognition for performance* – this is non-financial as well as financial.
- *Working for an organization of which the employee is proud.* This sense of pride may result from the organization's purpose, success, ethics, the quality of its leadership or the quality and impact of its products.

Camaraderie

The third goal of employees is to have warm, interesting and cooperative relations with others in the workplace. The most significant aspects of camaraderie are, in priority order:

1. Relationships with co-workers.
2. Teamwork within a worker's business unit.
3. Teamwork across departments in a specific location.
4. Teamwork and cooperation across the entire organization.

Engagement and the three factors

There are several other key points about the three-factor theory. First, employee enthusiasm (a state of high employee morale that derives from satisfying the three needs of workers) results in significant competitive advantage for those companies with the strength of leadership to manage for the long-term.

Also, people and their morale matter tremendously for all aspects of business success, including customer satisfaction. Employee morale is a function of the way an organization is led and the way that leadership is translated into daily management practices.

Finally, success breeds success: the better the individual and organization perform, the greater is employee morale, which, in turn, improves and sustains performance. It does not matter which one comes first; it is a virtuous cycle and wherever you start success will follow: morale drives performance and performance enhances morale. The challenge is to ensure that managers understand the connection.

The extent to which these three factors hold true for everyone is less important than the fact that they matter a great deal, to many people. The challenge, therefore, is to manage people in ways that take account of the need for employee engagement.

Checklist: connecting employee enthusiasm with business success
Having seen what workers want and why it matters, one vital question remains, what practical action should HR professionals take to facilitate employee enthusiasm and deliver stronger performance? The first, central point is that there is no single, simple answer – no silver bullet or magic formula for success. What is needed is the practical application of common sense and diligence, combined with genuine insights into the issues. Specific, practical steps can also be taken to ensure that enthusiasm is maintained and connected with business success.

Assess whether HR is complicit, perhaps unwittingly,
in destroying enthusiasm
Consider the extent to which your organization's existing policies reduce engagement. For example, do policies and procedures encourage achievement and develop camaraderie? What policies and procedures could be abandoned?

We need to recognize that company policies are designed to police the 5% of employees who need policing, yet they may significantly antagonise or discourage the 95% of employees who do not.

Also, do the organization's policies and procedures create equity, encourage achievement and develop camaraderie in the workplace? Equity is the most important factor in shaping employee enthusiasm. Data shows that when equity is rated low, even if achievement and camaraderie are rated high overall enthusiasm can be up to two-thirds lower. Fortunately, equity is largely in the domain of HR: it concerns the employment policies, procedures and working practices. So, HR can play an important role by auditing company policies.

• What policies and procedures could be abandoned? Often, company policies are designed to police the 5% of employees who need policing, yet they may significantly antagonize or discourage the 95% of employees who do not.

• Consider what new programmes should be introduced, and base these programmes on a clear understanding of your employees. For example, gainsharing (a method for ensuring that the gains that employees themselves achieve for the organization are shared with those employees) may help to ensure equity and encourage camaraderie.

Ensure managers realize the significance of equity, achievement and camaraderie, and that they routinely reflect this understanding in their actions.

The most effective way to do this is to simply highlight the connection between these issues and the business outcomes for which they are accountable. HR can enhance this awareness through management training, coaching and selection.

Survey employees regularly, using a consistent set of questions across the organization

Even if awareness is raised among managers, there are two potential problems. First, managers may forget the significance of these three factors or else simply fail to realize that they are constantly relevant. Second, the relative importance of each of the three factors and how employees perceive them will constantly alter. The solution is to understand that employee enthusiasm is a shifting aspect of organizational life and that practical action needs to be taken regularly.

- Regularly provide survey data and disaggregate it into organizational units, making it accessible to individual managers and supervisors.
- Organize the survey data and questions around the three basic needs. Use questions that test the dimensions of equity, achievement and camaraderie.
- Conduct linkage analysis to clearly assess which factors are affecting employee enthusiasm (the strength and direction of the correlations between certain attitudinal dimensions and business outcomes – such as productivity, profitability, safety or innovation).
- Consider introducing a common set of standards against which business unit performance is measured. This can be in the form of an index of items that most strongly correlate to commitment and engagement.
- Hold managers accountable for improvement.

Find the areas for intervention – good and bad practice

While few organizations have universally high enthusiasm, most have 'pockets of excellence' – departments or units where scores are high. Find out what the managers in these pockets are doing to create such high morale and leverage these insights across the organization.

- Consider teaming a high scoring manager with a couple of low scoring supervisors.
- Organize peer group review and challenge the group to raise the overall average score for units within that peer group.

Parts of the organization with low scores on employee enthusiasm should be helped, and the 'three factor' approach provides a practical focus with which to understand what is happening and what action should be taken. For example, a survey will reveal if the problem lies predominantly with equity, achievement or camaraderie. In those areas where there are problems, HR can help managers pinpoint the root causes and adopt solutions to reduce their effects.

Develop teamwork

Teamwork is a fundamental part of business life; fortunately, data shows that most individuals want to work in teams. So, by fostering teamwork and collaboration, we address two essential aspects of camaraderie. Yet even within teams, the need for equity and achievement must not be ignored. It may help to remind managers that leading a high performing team involves:

• Setting the context for the team, in terms of why it has been formed and what challenges it needs to address.
• Providing a suitable framework for people, setting the boundaries within which they will work and the direction they will take, and ensuring that they understand both.
• Ensuring the team then develops a shared sense of the goal they are pursuing. Have them identify all the possibilities within the framework provided; select the most significant opportunity and then commit to actions.
• Encouraging active participation in activities and decision-making.
• Empowering team members within agreed limits.
• Demonstrating the standards of behaviour that are expected from the team and ensuring equitable treatment.
• Defending the team from external disruption.

Manage and resolve conflicts between individuals

Conflict between co-workers is a major challenge to employee enthusiasm. While conflict may have many causes it often springs from inequity – for example, if an individual is perceived not to be contributing fully by co-workers. Common sense approaches include encouraging managers to talk to each person individually, establish the facts and come to a quick judgement about necessary actions.

When poor performance cannot be resolved

Sometimes there are cases when individuals are simply unable to step up their performance. It is important to distinguish the root cause of this – is it skill or will? Take steps to put a formal improvement plan in place and be prepared to take action if progress is not made. Practically, employ a 'three strikes and out' approach to get the individual back on track. How you are seen to deal with this is incredibly important not just for the individual concerned but also for the wider team and the culture you are trying to create. We have both worked in organizations where although poor performance was dealt with swiftly – and the individual concerned was paid off, they simply disappeared from the office. This type of macho approach to performance can over time build a culture of fear across the organization. People are embarrassed to talk about this and many secretly fear that the same might happen to them.

We recommend moving people on from the team or the organization in an upfront way. Clearly sensitivity is required around each individual circumstance, however it is important to acknowledge the contribution they have made, however small, and support them to their next transition. An 'elegant exit' says a great deal about you as a leader and it is key to strengthening the engagement of other employees.

Face up to poor performance and focus on partnership building

Typically, over 40% of survey respondents believe that companies do either 'too little' or 'much too little' to face up to poor performance (this percentage does not change materially between union and non-union organizations). In this situation firms can choose one of several approaches: conflict management aimed at reducing the costs of conflict; partnership building where managers work as allies for the greater good – or ostrich management, where the problem is ignored. Of these, data shows that partnership building is the most effective and durable.

The key components and characteristics of a partnership organization have been known for many years, but it is worth restating some of them to remind ourselves of these basic principles:

- *Win-Win:* The parties recognize that they have key business goals in common and that the success of one party depends on the success of the other. Reward practice should reflect this principle.

- *Basic trust:* Employees learn to trust the word of their leaders and management acknowledges the contribution of employees, wherever it occurs.
- *Long-term perspective:* The company is committed to a long-term relationship, one that will survive the short-term vicissitudes of business. While few organizations can realistically commit to life-time employment, the clear expression of intent to use redundancies only as a last resort can create a strong bond with employees. This was highlighted by the example of SouthWest Airlines, whose refusal to lay-off employees in the aftermath of the severe business downturn post September 11th 2001 provided a source of competitive advantage for the business.
- *Excellence:* The parties set high performance standards for themselves and for each other. Successful companies like BP are renowned for their high standards – up and down the organizational hierarchy.
- *Joint decision-making:* To the greatest extent practical, the parties make key decisions jointly on matters that affect each of them – particularly in a unionized environment.
- *Open communications:* The parties communicate with each other fully (and not just when there is bad news to share).
- *Day-to-day treatment:* The parties routinely treat each other with consideration and respect. Managers who score low in this area should be helped to improve their behaviour, or removed if they fail to improve.
- *Financial sharing:* To the extent that the collaboration is designed to generate improved financial results, the parties share equitably in those results. *Gainsharing* programmes reinforce this principle.

Let shareholders and analysts know the facts

If morale has improved and benchmarks well against other comparable organizations, incorporate the data in the company's annual report. Not only will it serve to back-up the assertion that employees are the firm's greatest asset but it will also inform investors and potential recruits about the way you view employee enthusiasm.

There are several interesting conclusions from Sirota's work that are worth highlighting. First, his firm's extensive research highlights a clear correlation between employee enthusiasm and organizational performance.

Employee enthusiasm (a state of high employee morale) results in significant competitive advantages for those organizations choosing to manage for long-term results.

Also, Sirota's research reveals that little real conflict exists between the goals of the overwhelming majority of workers and those of their employees. People and their organizations are not in a state of perpetual hostility – and it is harmful to think they are. The key question is not how to motivate employees but how to sustain the motivation that employees naturally bring to their jobs. Assessing employee enthusiasm is a vital aspect of retaining and managing talent. Whilst employee enthusiasm directly affects performance overall, a significant benefit of a clear focus on this issue is the opportunity to measure, manage and develop the enthusiasm of the organization's most talented employees.

Next, managing equity, achievement and camaraderie can only be done with a clear understanding of the priority actions needed, and with the active support of senior executives at the top of the organization. These require a segmented approach leading to an understanding not only of what people feel but why.

Finally, it is worth reflecting on the sad fact that despite this correlation between employee enthusiasm and organizational performance being widely accepted and acknowledged, relatively few firms take the right action to enhance employee enthusiasm. This may result from either a lack of understanding of the specific significance of equity, achievement and camaraderie, or from a simple belief among senior executives that this link does not exist. The issue for HR professionals is clear: if you accept the link between enthusiasm and performance, is your organization doing all it can to enhance employee enthusiasm?

The rule of 150: Gore Associates

Another interesting approach to the perennial challenge of getting people to perform well and collaborate is provided by Gore Associates, a privately held, multi-million dollar high-tech firm based in Delaware. As well as manufacturing the water-resistant Gore-Tex fabric, the firm also produces everything from insulating cables to dental floss, focusing on products for the semiconductor, pharmaceutical and medical industries.

Gore is unique because of their adherence to the rule of 150. This approach is based on anthropological research highlighting the fact that humans can socialize in large groups because, uniquely, we are able to handle the complexities of social arrangements. However, there is a limit to the bonds people can make and this is reached at around 150. In groups larger than 150, complicated hierarchies, regulations and formal measures are needed, but below 150 these same goals can be achieved informally.

Consequently, Gore limits the size of each office so it is below 150. Gore has fifteen plants within a twelve-mile radius in Delaware and Maryland, each with a close-knit group of employees who understand each other and work well together. This approach emphasizes the benefits of collective management such as communication, initiative and flexibility and it has enabled a big business with thousands of employees to retain the attitude of a small, entrepreneurial start-up. The result is a rate of employee turnover that is a third of the industry average and sustained profitability and growth for over 35 years. The firm realized that co-workers find socializing, teamworking and associated activities, such as innovating, collaborating and sharing knowledge, much easier to achieve when they are placed in groups of less than 150 (perhaps proving Sirota's point about the significance of camaraderie). In this way, a large corporation like Gore can gain the benefit of smaller groups that are often closer, more energetic, entrepreneurial, supportive and better.

Gore has taken several steps to make sure this approach works. They have divided their workforce into groups or branches of under 150 people, and instituted a strong managerial system to oversee smaller 'branches' and ensure they are coordinated and efficient. They also encourage a sense of community and teamwork within groups. The 'rule of 150' simply means that it will be possible for workers to form positive bonds with all of their co-workers – extra measures should be taken to ensure that this actually happens. Finally, the firm makes sure that they develop a sense of team *across* groups of 150. This means finding ways for people to communicate and collaborate across the whole business, rather than developing a series of competitive, separate groupings.

Sears and the service-profit chain

Senior executives at the US-based retailer Sears realized in the early-1990s that future performance was not going to be enhanced simply by developing a different strategy or adjusting their marketing plans. The firm was running significant losses – what was required was a thorough understanding of three issues:

- How employees felt about working at Sears.
- How employee behaviour affected customers' shopping experience.
- How customers' shopping experience affected profits.

On a single day, Sears asked 10% of their workforce – 30,000 employees – how much profit they thought the firm made for each dollar sold. The average answer was 46 cents, whereas in reality the answer was *1 cent*. This highlighted the need for employees, and especially those at the front line, to better understand the issues determining profitability and success. Sears' response was to make clear the chain of cause and effect. Because employees were better able to see the implications of their actions, it changed the way they thought and acted – and this, in turn, was reflected in bottom-line performance.

US retailer Sears provides one of the best examples of how employee engagement directly affects business performance. The service profit chain makes explicit the links between cause and effect. By enabling employees to see the implications of their actions, it can change the way people think and the results they achieve.

The starting point for the Service Profit Chain is the view that what is required for market leadership is an emphasis on managing *value drivers* – the aspects of the business that make the greatest difference and provide most benefit to customers. Of these value drivers, employee retention, employee satisfaction and employee productivity determine customer loyalty, revenue growth and profitability. This is shown below in the Service Profit Chain.

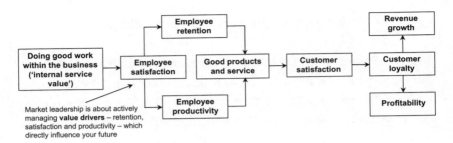

The Service Profit Chain

Another approach to measuring the link between investments in people and the firm's resulting performance is provided by the UK home depot retailer B&Q and their Employee Engagement Programme. This puts employee engagement and customer loyalty at the top of the agenda. With the B&Q approach, every manager has a regular, one-page report summarizing their performance in two areas: managing human capital and managing traditional finance measures. As a result of B&Q's programme, employee turnover reduced from 35% to 28% (each extra percentage point cost the company at least £1m) and profits increased, with turnover per employee rising by more than 20% within four years.

However, there is one point to remember, now and throughout this book: leadership is about balancing data and 'hard' process skills with 'softer' people-oriented skills – building trust and inspiration, guiding, communicating, developing an understanding of people, building relationships, and creating a positive climate in which people work.

Creating a climate for engagement

Having considered the benefits of engagement and the issues that influence it, it is worth understanding what great employee engagement looks like. In particular, how can you create a climate that engages the greatest possible number of your people – getting them to do more and go further than even they might have thought possible – and enables them to release what we call their *discretionary potential?* What are the rules, what is the right mindset or approach, and where are the potential pitfalls?

Understanding what doesn't work

First, we can be clear about what does *not* work. Engagement, like trust and other aspects of leadership and life, is not a coat, a temporary 'quick fix' approach that we can use when it suits us and discard when we choose. It is a genuine belief system. We don't engage or encourage people for our own narrow personal gain. We engage people because we are genuinely interested in working with them and achieving something together. Proving this point is the answer to a question we have asked many senior executives and leaders over many years: what are the top three qualities of a successful leader? Time and again one answer features in their replies: *you have to like people*. It seems highly likely (and plausible) that no leader ever achieved the benefits of engagement or ensured that people were working at their best, without having a genuine interest or connection with the people around them.

Also, engagement is not simply a set of tools and techniques that we can apply when we think they're needed. Certainly, there are useful techniques that can help get people on board and enthused (these are discussed below), and there are significant issues to bear in mind, but engaging with people is a state of mind – an approach – not a toolkit.

This links with the next point: the need to be positive about the people around you: striving to consider their situation, developing their skills, enabling them to achieve the goals that you and the organization have set, as well as their own personal goals. This is not 'soft' or indulgent: it's how to get the most from people by working with human nature. Of course, bullying and aggression can undeniably produce results but these are fragile and limited and the approach is unsustainable and short-term at best.

Getting people engaged

An example of an engaging, trusted and highly effective leader is Carlos Ghosn, President and CEO of Nissan and Renault. Born in Brazil in 1954, he became Renault's CEO in 2005 (he had become CEO of Nissan in 1999 when the carmakers formed an alliance). In Japan, he presided over the revival of Nissan. Carlos Ghosn identifies four vital elements of trusted leadership, particularly during a time of rapid global change:

- The ability to manage cross-culturally.
- A commitment to performance.
- Consistently living by clearly stated values.
- Transparency.

The ability to manage cross-culturally – getting the best out of people, whatever their nationality or background. This is particularly significant for a man facing the challenge of combining strong French and Japanese national cultures, but cross-cultural management also matters because globalization involves associating with people (most notably customers) of different cultures. Valuing cultural differences engenders rapport that in turn develops trust. Ghosn identifies the ability to 'exchange best practices, without any one culture being considered as the reference' as a critical factor both for performance and for achieving trust, motivation and commitment, he says.*

A commitment to performance is another essential element of corporate leadership, informing an organization's strategy, choices and key decisions. This involves not just short-term performance but all aspects determining future financial strength. In short, if customers, shareholders, employees, partners and suppliers trust the organization's commitment to do well, as made explicit in their strategy and actions, then success is more likely.

Consistently living by clearly stated values. Too often, leaders espouse corporate values or missions, only to compromise or ditch them when times change. Carlos Ghosn believes that living by stated values is particularly important during times of change, and he cites the example of the Renault-Nissan alliance. The stated priority at the time was to boost performance through synergies between the two companies, whilst at the same time he stressed the importance of keeping their separate brand identities, which were key assets. This was initially viewed with deep scepticism, yet Carlos Ghosn believes that one of the reasons the alliance

---

*Quotations from Carlos Ghosn are reported by the Economist Intelligence Unit in their article *CEO Agenda: Carlos Ghosn on Leadership*, published on www.eiu.com, 29 October 2002.

succeeded so quickly is because people recognized that everything was done according to these consistently and clearly stated values.

When it came to challenging past practices and attitudes, one of the toughest leadership tasks, consistent and clearly stated values were vitally important here as well. Within Nissan Carlos Ghosn was able to challenge many Japanese corporate traditions by putting the aim of improving performance above other values, such as lifetime employment or the long-standing seniority system for promotions. According to Carlos Ghosn: 'As long as people know that you're sticking to stated values, they accept it'.

Transparency is closely linked with trusted leadership, and to Carlos Ghosn this means 'You say what you think and you do what you say'. Only a limited, brittle, paper-thin form of transparency can be achieved with regulation. Without a belief that executives are genuinely upholding the spirit as well as the rules of transparency, it will always be of very limited value and use. An example of transparency is provided by Nissan's revival plan, developed immediately Carlos Ghosn took over the reins. 'In October 1999 I said outright that we're going to reduce headcount by 21,000, close five plants in Japan and reduce the number of suppliers by 50%. But I explained why, I explained how and I explained for what benefit'. The leadership made specific promises for profitability and debt reduction, and promised to resign if these promises were not delivered. 'I don't say it was easy, but we announced outright that there would be some hard times, that we'd try to do everything we could to make it as soft as possible on people but that there were limits', Carlos Ghosn recalls. 'The fact that we did this openly from the beginning was the essential condition to make the plan successful and transform the company very quickly'.

Leadership reflections

People like to be engaged and involved and if this is forthcoming they do better and go further than if they are not engaged. (The opposite of engagement can be viewed as 'mushroom management', where people are fed dirt and kept in the dark.) Building engagement starts within – meaning that you need to genuinely want to engage with other people, understanding and valuing interaction. The questions below are designed to help you develop the right approach in your own mind, as well as moving on to the more practical aspects of engagement.

1. Develop a personal understanding of engagement. What does engagement mean to you? Why might it be of value to your organization, your team and yourself?

It may help you to reflect on a time when a project or situation involving several people worked really well and people were engaged. What were the factors or conditions that lead to this engagement? What was achieved by people who were enthused and engaged? How did they work and what were their accomplishments?

2. Understand your relationships and constituents. Who are the people that you need to engage with? Are your relationships with these people strong enough for you to succeed? Crucially, how can you build and strengthen these relationships?

To help you answer these questions it may help to reflect on a successful interaction or conversation that you had with someone. How did it go – what was the pattern and tone of the interaction? What was the outcome? How did it feel? What would you do differently next time?

3. Decide the best approach. What type of engagement would work well in a specific situation?

The options vary considerably but may include, for example: *telling* people information; *selling* ideas, information or decisions to people; *including* people in certain, clearly-defined aspects of a situation, decision or process (for example, delegating specific tasks), or *collaborating* with people across a wide range of activities, seeking and benefiting from their views and generally working together and 'co-creating'.

4. Decide the scope and boundaries of engagement. How engaged – and in what way – do you want people to be with a specific situation or decision?

It is tempting to think of engagement as something that a leader does with their colleagues or team members, but some of the most interesting and powerful examples of engagement are provided by firms interacting and engaging with their customers. Harley-Davidson is one such example. From its beginnings in Milwaukee in 1909, Harley-Davidson has enjoyed a long history as the USA's foremost motorbike manufacturer. However, by the early 1980s their reputation and business were in serious trouble following a sustained onslaught from affordable, high quality Japanese machines produced by companies such as Honda and Kawasaki. Following a management buy-out, Harley-Davidson tackled their product quality problems using the production techniques of Dr W. Edwards Deming (ironically, an American whose quality methods transformed Japanese manufacturing). The next challenge was to win back – and maintain – market share. This they achieved, becoming America's leading bike manufacturer with an amazing 90% of Harley-Davidson customers staying loyal to the company.

There are several methods that Harley-Davidson uses to build trust and bond with their customers, and each one combines knowledge of individual customer's needs with a cleverly-judged appeal to their emotions. The result is that their customers trust them and they value this, using it to develop stronger bonds, greater profits and more trust, in a virtuous circle. For example, the managers of the business meet their customers regularly at rallies, where new models can be sampled with free demonstration rides. Also, the Harley Owner's Group (HOG) is a member loyalty programme with activities that bind customers to the company, and rather than providing trite or cheap benefits Harley devotes considerable resources to ensuring that their customers receive benefits that they value. Membership of HOG is free for the first year for new Harley owners, thereafter a membership fee (approximately $40) is payable – and over two-thirds of customers renew. Throughout the 1990s and into the 2000s Harley-Davidson achieved steady year-on-year growth, with record revenues and earnings.

Rich Teerlink, former Chairman and CEO of Harley-Davidson, highlights two factors contributing to the firm's successful renaissance. 'Perhaps the most significant program was – and continues to be – the Harley Owners Group (HOG), created in 1983. Begun as a way to communicate more effectively with the company's end users, HOG quickly grew into the world's largest motorcycle club. And dealers [a vital customer group and sales channel] regained confidence that Harley could and would be a dependable partner'. The second factor highlighted by Teerlink was the company's willingness and ability to unleash the ideas of their people. 'I myself didn't have a plan for the company in my back pocket. I only knew that capturing the ideas of our people – all the people at Harley – was critical to our future success'.

It might seem easy to sell a product as exciting and appealing as a motorbike. But then Harley-Davidson also manages to get tens of thousands of their customers to keep on buying their machines, as well as paying to attend rallies where they enjoy themselves, make friends, provide valuable customer feedback – and even tattoo themselves with the name of the company. How many businesses do you know that can achieve that?

5.   Get engaged in the right way, at the right time. What is the best way for you to get people engaged and enthused? If successful, the preceding questions should get you to the point where engaging people is simple and easy (as it should be). Several practical techniques can help to get people engaged and, more generally, to develop a culture of engagement. These include:

- developing empathy;
- empowering people;
- being self-aware;
- coaching and developing people;
- communicating (by which we mean asking, listening, explaining and taking and coordinating action with an enhanced level of understanding);
- inspiring trust.

In the next chapter we broaden discussion about engagement and consider the connection between leadership and talent. In particular we consider what, in addition to engagement, are the priorities for a twenty-first century leader? What are the forces shaping leadership? The answers will help to highlight how we can attract people to work for us and how we can help them realize their potential.

Chapter 8

The Meaning of Work

Every one of us can send emails on Sunday night, but how many of us know how to go to the movies on Monday afternoon? If you don't know how to go to the movies from 2 to 4, you're in trouble because you've just taken on something that unbalances life, but you haven't rebalanced it with something else.

Ricardo Semler's 'Leading by omission' speech at MIT Sloan
School of Management

The meaning of work

In most organizations, people wish to leave it better than when they arrived: they aspire to deliver quality as well as achieve recognition and reward. This should come as no surprise; after all, very few successful people are content simply to work on a pointless endeavour for long. Proving this point is Pearson, the largest education company in the world with some of the strong-

Getting the best from talented people (or most people) is best achieved by giving people work which has meaning.

est brands in business information and consumer publishing, including the *Financial Times*, Penguin and Pearson itself. Senior Pearson executives go out of their way to explain to their managers how the business started, how it has come to be successful and what makes it special. In particular, talented Pearson managers gather every year from around the world for a meeting which, among other issues, is also an opportunity to explain the history of the business. This in turn helps people understand and appreciate Pearson's culture and values – and it's an inspiring, instructive story.

Weetman Pearson was born in July 1856 in Yorkshire, in the north of England. His grandfather Samuel started the firm known today as Pearson in 1844 and for many years the firm focused on construction, eventually becoming one of the world's largest construction companies with most of its operations outside the UK.

Aged 17 and having already run one of his father's businesses in England, Weetman Pearson spent a year in the USA in 1876. It was a formative experience that prepared him well for building the world's largest construction company, as well as laying the foundations for today's Pearson. Impressed with America's infectious energy and enthusiasm, Weetman Pearson came to learn two lessons that are as relevant today as they were in the past: don't ask people to do things you would not do yourself, and treat others as you would like to be treated. He took this advice to great lengths, physically helping to construct some of the projects being built by his company. These exertions left him in hospital more than once.

An early supporter of globalization, Weetman Pearson took over the company in 1880, at the ripe old age of 24. The business that he developed built Dover harbour as well as railroads and major civil engineering projects around the world. In 1889, Porfirio Diaz invited him to Mexico to build a railroad from the Atlantic to the Pacific. While laying track, his crew discovered one of the world's largest oil fields, the Potrero del Llano. He created the Mexican Eagle Petroleum Company, one of Mexico's largest firms. It was taken over by the Royal Dutch Petroleum Company (now Royal Dutch Shell) in 1919.

After 1918, Pearson bought several newspapers and it was these, together with his values and approach to business, which laid the foundation for the company of today. He treated his employees with care and generosity, understanding that people needed to be encouraged and directed if they were to give their best. Uncaring, unthinking brutality at work would be ultimately self-defeating. Of course, this is a concept about business that civilized societies have come to understand and now enshrine in law, but in Weetman Pearson's world of the nineteenth and early twentieth centuries – and in the rough world of construction – it was quite a departure from the norm. For example, he was the first employer to provide his workers with pensions and he also believed in employee share ownership.

Combined with Pearson's international approach was a strong sense of entrepreneurship, commercialism and values. It mattered to Pearson that his business was being built on a firm set of principles. Weetman Pearson understood that it is possible to be honourable, honest and profitable. After serving as a member of parliament, including a spell in the wartime government of David Lloyd George in 1917 where he was responsible for aircraft production, Pearson eventually retired and died in May 1927. His obituary highlighted his 'daring, originality and ingenuity', while his own philosophy emphasized perseverance and patience. All of these qualities remain hallmarks of today's Pearson.

From the 1960s onwards the company that Pearson had built began to focus even more on publishing, eventually growing into one of the world's most successful publishers. This shift from one industry to another may seem strange but it is by no means unique – other major corporations such as Nokia have similarly shifted their focus (in Nokia's case, from timber to mobile telephony). Pearson's story suggests that what matters most is not simply what the company does, or its size or even the company's output, vital though these things are. What matters to its employees and, ultimately, its customers, is *who* it is. Weetman Pearson was certainly not a saint, but anyone who hears the Pearson story being told cannot fail to be impressed by the tale of a brave, enterprising, visionary and decent young man who simply enjoyed his work and let his personality shine through. Ultimately, he gave the company the character and culture it has today, a character that seems to have survived for more than a hundred years and has spanned a diverse range of industries, countries and challenges.

Pearson executives today use the story to remind their managers of the company's character and values: for Pearson, these are to be brave, imaginative and decent. Now, many firms espouse high-minded values that can seem to their employees to be vacuous, but set in the context of a past that includes Weetman Pearson's priorities and style, and a present position as one of the world's largest publishers and education businesses, these values have real meaning to people at Pearson. This is how one of Weetman

Pearson's legacies – the firm's values – were described in 2009, 82 years after his death:

- Brave – being willing to drive forward with energy and determination is vital. Bravery also means doing things you never thought you would do.
- Imaginative – this is what Pearson is all about: connecting with people and being thoughtful and creative in all that we do.
- Decent – people at Pearson should follow Weetman Pearson's example and treat others as they would wish to be treated. Being decent also means erring on the side of generosity.

Pearson succeeds by giving its employees' work real *meaning*. Today, for example, the company is hugely proud of the fact that it is working in Angola to produce textbooks in seven indigenous languages, some of which have never previously had a single textbook. This isn't simple altruism: the firm employs 30,000 people worldwide and has made steady returns for its share-holders, despite sometimes challenging economic circumstances. Of course, the firm will inevitably make mistakes and do the wrong thing from time to time, just as a person might, but it's the character that counts and that can be shaped by the past as well as leadership in the present. Addressing a group of the firm's managers in 2008 Pearson's Chairman, Glen Moreno, commented: 'Successful global companies believe in what they do. They have a purpose'.

Is it just coincidence or happenstance that a company with this character and history – one that is tirelessly and proudly handed down from one set of managers to the next – is also a leader in several important and highly competitive industries (notably business information, educational and con-sumer publishing)? Surely it is much more likely that this corporate char-acter is attracting talented and enthusiastic people, inspiring and engaging them so they can truly excel and, ultimately, delivering great results (and not only commercially).

The equation is simple: for the most part, companies such as Pearson have a character and approach that gives meaning and value to their work; people (mostly employees) respond, and the business thrives. Making this happen in practice is, of course, the challenge of leadership.

The importance of meaningful work

Leaders will help themselves, their teams and their organizations if they appreciate that the changing nature of our economies has greatly influenced our lives as consumers and our expectations of work. Arguably however, the ghosts of the Industrial Age ethos, long hours, hard labour and deference are still alive in the system. The work environment has greatly lagged behind in the imagination stakes, so much so that it seems like we have forgotten the reason why as human beings we work in the first place; to do something meaningful.

This drive to achieve meaning through work has been described as a deeply rooted human instinct. It is about being able to apply your personal abilities, physically and imaginatively onto the world. This might be express to yourself, create something new or achieve a goal. In all cases something is different because of you —you have made a mark.

Psychologist Estelle Morin describes the importance of the work instinct and how doing meaningful work is vital in generating individual potential.

> When an individual does meaningful work, he actually develops a sense of identity, worth, and dignity. By achieving meaningful results, he actually achieves himself, grows, and even, actualizes his full potential. Somehow, he has an opportunity to become who he is and to contribute to the improvement of his life conditions and of his community.
>
> When one thinks of work, one often thinks of a job. But work is far more than a job. Although work certainly provides for basic subsistence needs and decent living conditions, this is not its only function. Work is, above all, an activity through which an individual fits into the world, creates new relations, uses his talents, learns, grows and develops his identity and a sense of belonging.

People – more than 'human resources'

Work, therefore, has an emotional and social purpose. We use it to connect to our personal potential and also to contribute to our wider society. And yet how much space is there for this to happen in today's workplace? We have job descriptions, competencies and roles all created with good intent: to tell us what to do and to tell us how to do it. While helpful to the uninitiated, we wonder how much these have neutered each individual's relationship with work. Where is the space to personalize our roles and shape how we deliver it? The danger is that we really are viewing people and individuals as 'human resources' – impersonal assets to be aggregated, rather than people to be managed and led.

We believe organizations have a tremendous amount of untapped potential and that the discretionary nature of this pivots entirely on how each individual is able to re-connect with their basic instinct for meaningful work.

Writers on employment relations have long asserted that we have traded this need for employment security. The need to feed our families and pay our rent (they argue) has driven a financial relationship between an employer and employee. The end of employment security in the 1980s has left this transactional relationship troubled. So much so that we believe along with the demographic challenge, this alienation from work is one of our key talent dilemmas.

Making work more meaningful

Meaning, of course, is a highly personal and subjective notion. It differs between individuals and at different life stages. Writers in this area have identified a number of factors influencing how individuals derive meaning from work. These can be summarized as:

- The significance that work brings to our sense of identity.
- The orientation we have towards work; specifically how we achieve our personal values. These may range from autonomy to social advancement.
- The balance we are able to achieve between work and other important aspects of our lives; family, friends etc....

We might move through each of these areas of importance as our careers progress or simply be motivated by one. The key is understanding how work becomes meaningful to each individual. Estelle Morin and her team have researched this internationally and established the following six factors that help work to become more meaningful:

Social purpose	Doing something that is useful to others or to society, that contributes to society.
Moral correctness	Doing a job that is morally justifiable in terms of its processes and its results.
Achievement-related pleasure	Enjoying one's job, doing a job that stimulates the development of one's potential and that enables achieving one's goals.
Autonomy	Being able to use one's skills and judgment to solve problems and make decisions regarding one's job.
Recognition	Doing a job that corresponds to one's skills, whose results are recognized and whose salary is adequate
Positive relationships	Doing a job that enables making interesting contacts and good networks

It is interesting to reflect how simple these are and how universal. There has been much made of the need to consider factors such as these for Generation Y, however we believe these are important wherever you are on the demographic timeline.

We believe the need to generate more potential in our workforce will drive a new psychological contract where employees will exchange their potential for meaning. We think in effect this already happens in the most successful workplaces. The more we feel able to work on stimulating projects, the more we are able to influence the way that we work, the quality of the relationships we enjoy with our colleagues and the pride we have in the organization, the better we'll perform. We'll understand feedback on how we can do better, if we understand how it'll make work more enjoyable or make a bigger impact.

Meaning is the force which gives rise to employees that are *engaged*; meaning determines how we differentiate one employer from another. The old employment contract is broken. Our workforces have long memories: each generation has now experienced recession or unemployment. You have an employment brand whether you like it or not – increasingly you have very little control over it.

Leadership reflections

- **Social purpose:** do people appreciate the value or impact of their work? If this work is menial or junior in status, do they really appreciate that they are part of a larger enterprise? This may not be relevant for everyone but meaningful, valuable work is much more widespread than most employees would imagine.
- In addition to a social purpose is the fact that people are often stimulated by the progress they are making for themselves and their organization – this progress may be in the form of financial or commercial gains.
- **Moral correctness:** are people managed at all times in a way that is morally correct? Is the content of their work morally justifiable in terms of its content and results? If it isn't, or if this ever lapses even temporarily, then most people will find it less rewarding or personally sustainable.
- **Achievement-related pleasure:** do people enjoy their work? Is there a feeling that people are developing their potential and achieving their goals? Is success clearly recognized and rewarded?
- **Autonomy:** are people able to work autonomously, bringing their own skills and judgement to the challenges of problem-solving and decision-making? Are people routinely guided by an understanding of their organization's vision, values and strategy?
- **Recognition:** are people able to use their full skills and experience? Are their interests and aspirations being recognized, valued and expanded? Is their remuneration fair?
- **Positive relationships:** are people able to connect with their colleagues and benefit from the stimulation of working with others? Are people working positively as in teams, for example, collaborating across organizational boundaries?

Also important is the need to avoid *fragmentation* and *groupthink* as both can corrode the meaning of work. Fragmentation occurs when people are in disagreement, either with their peers or their superiors. Usually, the expression of emerging dissent is disguised or suppressed, although it may appear as 'passive aggression'. Dissenting opinion often festers in the background – mentioned informally in conversation, rather than clearly raised in formal situations, such as meetings. Fragmentation is corrosive, hindering effective analysis and decision making, and can worsen when the views of one group dominate. It also feeds off itself in a self-sustaining cycle, as any move to break it is seen as an attempt to gain dominance by one side. It can therefore become locked-in to the organization and be extremely difficult to reverse.

Groupthink is the opposite of fragmentation. It occurs when the group suppresses ideas that are critical or not in support of the direction in which the group is moving. The group appears to be in agreement or certain but is neither. It is caused by many factors, such as past success breeding a belief in an infallible team and complacency. Groupthink may occur because the group is denied information or members lack the confidence or ability to challenge the dominant views of the group. People may be concerned about disagreeing, either because of past events, present concerns or a fear of what the future might hold, therefore seek safety in numbers.

There are several guiding principles that will help avoid these problems:

- Be bold and don't fear the consequences of decisions.
- Trust your instincts and emotions.
- Be prepared to play devil's advocate.
- Avoid irrelevancies.
- Reframe decisions, challenges or opportunities.
- Don't let the past hold you back.
- Challenge groupthink – people are often afraid to comment or to act because of social pressure. This is a poor excuse. Find out what people really think and use that to inform decisions.
- Take unpopular decisions when needed.
- Achieve consensus by agreeing the purpose of the decision.
- Gather the facts so you can accurately define and understand the issues.

Making work meaningful and getting employees engaged are two of the most significant leadership challenges. In the next chapter we consider the nature of leadership in the twenty-first century: what issues are important and how to ensure success.

Chapter 9

Leading for Talent

The metaphor of a perfect storm captures the current environment perfectly. We are witnessing the rare convergence of complexity and diversity, a convergence that challenges all our leadership assumptions. Imagine leaders as captains steering ships through this perfect storm. The old charts are outdated, and even the smartest strategists have not yet been able to adequately map a new world.

These are not times for average leaders or for those who cannot appreciate and use the skills of their key people. If this perfect storm is to be navigated, it will take whole leaders who use their full potential to move the enterprise through an enormously complex, diverse and uncertain era.

David L Dotlich, Peter C Cairo, Stephen H Rhinesmith
Leading in Times of Crisis, JosseyBass 2009

Outstanding leadership is an essential catalyst for talent. Leaders have the ability to shape the character of an organization and the experience individuals have of work. This will influence the type of people that are attracted to work with you and the career decisions of those already in your team. Most immediately it impacts on day-to-day performance; the extent to which people seek out new opportunities and the lengths they will go to deliver them.

The new world order has yet to settle; it has added a more ambiguous backdrop to how leaders operate. Each day demands a different perspective and a revised forecast. Structures change and lay offs become a necessary part of the organization's survival. Clients change and customers need more for less. Meanwhile, the cost of delivery continues to rise. This complexity and pace challenges the capacity of every leader (whatever their ability or experience) and requires a new approach to leading people; one where every individual has the insight and autonomy to make decisions and where they have the right skills to take action.

This is an evolutionary leap away from the idea of the leader as the most capable member of the team, towards the idea that the best leaders build the most capable teams. This means really getting to grips with each individual's ability and their aspiration for work; and an appreciation that these require daily maintenance. As we have previously discussed there is no cookie cutter template for this; it's got to be personal. Get it wrong and your people leave, or worse, they stay with you and stand on the sideline. How many times have you heard the phrase 'I joined an organization but left a line manager'? And, as a leader, how much of your energy goes into dealing with poor performance and when was the last time you had a weekend off?

Leading for talent means getting the best performance out of every single member of your team and teaching them how to get the best from each other. This requires a new set of leadership capabilities; understanding how to build trust, how to identify potential, how to build capability and how to let people go. Crucially, the first step requires that as a leader you better understand yourself, your style, and how you are able to adapt this.

In this chapter we ask you to reflect on your own leadership style and how this will influence your effectiveness as a leader for talent. In chapter 10 we provide a series of practical techniques for how you can do this in the workplace.

The challenges of 21st century leadership

Leadership is a contentious topic that fascinates and infuriates in equal measure. Everybody has their own view of leadership, and while there is a considerable amount of consensus on the topic there is also a great deal of confusion and, crucially, a decisive personal element as well. As if that weren't enough the topic of leadership is made even more complex by the presence of different leadership styles. And, perhaps more importantly, how leaders are able to adapt their style to the context they find themselves in and the people they work with.

All of this matters because growing and engaging talent is at the core of leadership – one of the truths about talent.

Ask people about what makes a good leader and they will tell you that they exercise good judgement, create opportunities and drive change. Most importantly, leaders display a range of characteristics; belief, vision, integrity and an ability to connect with others that makes people want to follow them.

These qualities are perennial. The only difficulty with these qualities and leadership in general is that they are too universal and broad. The issue of leadership can be seen as too amorphous, over-used and misunderstood, and it has become abused in recent years by political, religious and business leaders who have disappointed their constituents in ever-increasing numbers.

Instead, to lead in today's complex, fast-moving world it can help to view priorities as being in three main areas:

- setting and implementing strategy (this includes vision and direction);
- develop trusting relationships;
- consistently making decisions and doing the right thing based on personal values.

Leaders who partially achieve success in some or all of these areas may prosper in the short term but, over time, their organizations lose. Business writers David L. Dotlich, Peter C. Cairo and Stephen H. Rhinesmith highlight these three priorities in their book *Head, Heart and Guts: How the world's best companies develop complete leaders* (Jossey-Bass, 2006).

It may be worth repeating three vital issues that fundamentally affect leadership and the success of people and the organizations that employ them:

- We believe everyone has potential to be more talented; specifically an ability to create value
- Potential gets realized through meaningful work and good guidance
- You can't manage talent, you can only ask it to share with you

There are, of course, many attributes of great leaders but several issues are especially significant – and occasionally neglected – when leading people.

Before we explain about these three priorities for leaders (what David Dotlich and his colleagues call *head, heart* and *guts*) and how to make them work in practice, it is worth considering why these qualities are so significant today. In fact, for any leader wanting to engage with their people and help them realize their potential it helps to understand the impact of several trends and issues.

Globalization, interconnectedness and interdependence

To lead in today's complex, fast-moving world it can help leaders to view their priorities as being in three main areas: setting and implementing strategy, developing trusting relationships, and consistently making decisions and doing the right thing based on personal values.

Leaders need to operate with a 'broader-mind' and a wider perspective than ever before. There are new qualities that a generation ago were hardly considered; issues such as diversity, respect, humility and trust when dealing with people in different countries and cultures, as well as the need to manage ambiguity, and the ability to take risks in the face of greater uncertainty. This not only applies to employees but customers as well.

Globalization results both in opportunities and challenges, it liberates and constrains, it creates the largest markets ever known and allows the potential players to be smaller than ever. If the future business world has a greater number of paradoxes then globalization will spawn many of them. So, what are the forces arising from globalization that affect leaders?

First, power is increasingly out of proportion to size. What matters in the global, connected economy is not simply size but other factors such as scarcity or reputation. Organizations that have intangible resources of loyalty, teamwork and engagement are more likely to turn those qualities into innovative, scarce and valuable products. Previously that scarcity was competed for only within a local or national market, now the potential demand is much bigger. So either the price rises or the volumes increase: either way the business benefits. Microsoft is a clear example. A business established in the mid-1970s now supports millions of enterprises and individuals with its software, while its revenues and profits dwarf the income of several nation states. It continues to do so not simply because it is now huge and has developed a powerful position in the market, but largely because of its intellectual property, brand recognition and reputation.

Also, the developments behind globalization, notably in technology, require that leaders act swiftly and flexibly if they are to stay ahead of the competition. People have been able to travel the world for the past 500 years; the difference now is that they are connected immediately. The internet boom has made people realize that business could operate, more or less unconstrained by geography, 24 hours a day, 7 days a week and 365 days a year. This new, faster-moving, faster-changing business environment has driven companies of all sizes to organize themselves into smaller, more responsive, focused units. For example, affected by increasing competition in their global market, logistics firms such as DHL, UPS and FedEx have responded by enabling their customers to track their packages as they are transported. For large companies whose sheer size makes them more diffi-cult to manage, it can be hard to make themselves as flexible and responsive as smaller units are able to be.

Another issue for leaders to contend with resulting from increased glo-balization is that, paradoxically, people are reasserting tribal behaviour. In his book *Global Paradox* John Naisbitt argues that the more we become eco-nomically interdependent, the more we hold on to what constitutes our core basic identity. Fearing globalization and, by implication, a homogenized Western (predominantly American) culture, such countries as Indonesia, Russia and France have passed laws to preserve their distinctiveness and identity. This change may be neither uniform nor as powerful as some believe. Mankind is gregarious; valuing community and the ability to share information and form allegiances across borders can all reduce tribalism. But cultural issues run deep and must be taken into account by leaders. The merger of Daimler, a German automotive firm, and US-based Chrysler highlighted huge cross-cultural problems of organizational and manage-ment culture, and, by all accounts, there was much tribalism to contend with as well.

Globalization has also led to the realization that there are talented people, customers and markets well beyond the traditional Western company spheres of operation. For the majority of the twentieth century poor countries remained poor and rich countries remained rich. If a country's fortunes changed, then typically it occurred over decades. Now, societies develop skills, wealth and commercial opportunity in a much shorter time. For example, in the early 1960s, South Korea's GDP was on a par with that of present-day Sudan. In 1945, Japan and Germany were physically destroyed and largely friendless in the arena of international trade and long-term development. Within a generation, they had become the second and third richest countries in the world. Although the economic performance of both countries currently lags behind others, they remain among the five largest economies and enjoy the best standards of living. Conversely, at the start of the twentieth century Argentina was a leading economic power, whereas at the start of the twenty-first century it was in economic disarray and decline. The point is that international sources of strength and capability change.

At a time of business globalization and the apparent convergence of cultures at the surface level – with universal brands such as Sony, McDonald's, IKEA and CNN – successful leaders and organizations also allow for increased variety and differentiation. Global interdependence requires leaders to ask: how can I understand the values that are held by others? How can I relate these to my values? How do we then share understanding of these, building a successful working relationship?

Increasing complexity

More and more, people need to be engaged with their work if they are to be successful and fulfilled. Creating a motivating environment and motivating people to do things needs an explanation to win their minds and inspiration to win their hearts. An interesting example of the increasing complexity of work and the measures organizations will take to succeed is provided by the retailing sector. In this globally competitive industry, gone are the days when entrepreneurs such as Jesse Boot in Nottingham, Marcus Sieff in London and Sam Walton in Little Rock simply stacked their shelves with appealing products and threw open the shop doors. The US retailer Sears connects employee engagement directly with organizational performance with their employee-customer-profit chain. By enabling employees to see the implications of their actions, it can change the way people think and the results they achieve, making explicit the links between cause and effect.

The challenge of sustainable growth

It's important for you to know that you don't have to make a choice between owning a company that puts up great numbers and a company that is socially responsible. You own both.

Jack Welch in his address at the 1999 General Electric Annual Meeting, Cleveland, Ohio

Another issue shaping leadership in the twenty-first century is the need for growth. During the last decade this relentless pressure has resulted in some of the highest profile scandals in corporate history, with once-respected firms such as Enron coming crashing down to earth. Many other businesses, notably Lehman Brothers and other financial services firms as well as businesses in industries as diverse as auto-manufacturing and airlines, have focused simply on short-term growth and the next quarter's results, with disastrous consequences. Clearly, what is needed is more than an appeal-ing strategy. For people to contribute their commitment, effort and innovative thinking, leaders must help them believe in the vision, and that vision needs to be positive – ethically as well as commercially robust.

For people to contribute their commitment, effort and innovative thinking, leaders must help them believe in the vision, and that vision needs to be positive – ethically as well as commercially robust.

The Innocent Drinks Company epitomizes many of the characteristics of a firm that takes a positive, engaging approach to the challenge of growth. It produces high-quality fruit drinks and smoothies with a passion, profes-sionalism and good humour that invite trust. This tone is set from the top. Like many trusted leaders, executives like Innocent Drinks' founder Richard Reed do not spend much time focusing on trust. Instead, they simply display the energy and skills that people (employees and customers) value – and trust follows. This avoids the paradox of trust, where the more it is discussed the weaker it becomes.

The Innocent ethos developed by Reed and his colleagues in 2003 has been developed and honed by a clear vision and indelible principles:

procuring ethically, reducing and offsetting carbon emissions, recycling and putting something back through charitable giving. Innocent's fruit suppliers have to meet minimum International Labour Organization standards and premium rates are paid to Rainforest Alliance-accredited or local farms. Electricity comes from green renewable sources. Fleet vehicles are powered either by bio fuels, LPG or hybrid. CO_2 emissions are measured each month and are offset by 120% to be carbon negative across the business. And these are just a few of the ways that the firm works to meet the aspirations of its employees and consumers. As if that were not enough 10% of the firm's profit goes into community projects through the Innocent Foundation, which administers grants for communities in fruit source countries. This is both a business that is enjoying its work and is commercially-astute. Brand-building, recruitment, retention and sales are all linked to the ethos and all employees must be imbued with the right traits.

In the view of Richard Reed: 'We're about growth and profit as a business. Our people have to be equally commercial and altruistic', he says. 'It's a hard mix to find because people tend to over-index in one. They're either too far off in hippy-dom or too far off in Wall Street. But find them, incentivize, reward and encourage them to deliver in these areas and it's dynamite'. (See http://www.growingbusiness.co.uk/innocent-drinks-richard-reed.html.) (Reproduced by permission of Crimson Publishing.) This approach clearly succeeds, with Innocent Drinks enjoying a massive share in excess of 50% in its home market. Their success has been significant enough for Coca-Cola to take a 20% stake in the firm in 2009, enabling Innocent to expand in Europe and endorsing the firm's approach as a way to achieve future growth.

The need for innovation

One of the greatest challenges for leaders is to create a climate of innovation where people are not inhibited by fears, are eager to share ideas with others, and are keen to find and integrate new ideas. One firm that has had more success at this than most is Google, one of the twenty-first century's most successful businesses, dominating the market for online searching and advertizing. At times it is hard to discern which aspect of their business is most innovative: their ambition and ability to organize the world's informa-tion, or their commercial ability to make money from their services. In fact, both are vital and reflect an important feature of the business: a climate of innovation.

Crucially, employees at Google have the authority to act on their own initiative and are encouraged to make improvements and work on new developments. The result is that the firm is able to attract and retain driven people who enjoy improving and developing things and who value their freedom and autonomy. This situation then becomes a self-sustaining cycle: autonomy and empowerment lead to success and attract more talented people, and these people are then encouraged and empowered to succeed.

Also, it can be argued that one of Google's greatest strengths is their ability to recognize the value of failure and chaos. This is shown, most notably, by their approach to product development which releases a wide range of products with the expectation that some will become blockbusters. (Clearly, this also relies on an ability to spot and then maximize a blockbuster as soon as it appears.) This way of working provides valuable insights that can then be fed back into future developments. As well as directly resulting in new products, the creative frenzy also has the indirect benefit of building a culture that is not only innovative but also dynamic, well-informed and determined.

Changing attitudes, rising expectations

Another challenge for leaders is to recognize that now, more than ever before, employees have rising expectations. In particular, they are more sophisticated and better informed, and they expect more than a one-dimensional leader, someone who can navigate in an environment of danger and uncertainty.

The past fifty years have brought greater education, greater freedom of expression and thought, more equality, the erosion of traditional hierarchies and deference, greater social and geographic mobility of labour and many other social changes. A century ago, millions of people worked in large and intimidating

The world of work is changing significantly – it often has and, at least for the foreseeable future, this will continue. In coming years, for example, many Western firms will be challenged by a wave of retirements as baby boomers leave the workforce. In 2012 nearly one American worker in three will be over 50.

factories, accepting the hierarchical and paternalistic management structure. They formed unions to protect their rights and their livelihood. Managers directed and controlled on a mass scale and the art and science of management took shape. When commanded to fight and, if necessary, die during two world wars, people did. Today, unions are weaker, factories employ considerably fewer people, those that are employed are more skilled and educated, hierarchies are flatter and loyalties to employers and other institutions are less strong. For example, it is difficult to imagine millions of conscripted people in the developed world marching to war as they did twice in the twentieth century – and not just because the nature of warfare has changed. In the workplace, social change has necessitated an ability to manage change, show leadership, build teams, be innovative, manage knowledge and allow flexible working in order to benefit both organizations and those who work for them.

In addition, more women are employed than ever before and many want flexible careers. They are not alone: men also want greater flexibility. Demographic trends in developed countries indicate that populations are ageing; increasingly some people choose (or need) to work past traditional retirement ages – often part-time.

Looking beyond the developed world, corporations are adopting the different views of developing world economies. During the latter half of the twentieth century, the prevailing business logic was that nations such as India, China, Brazil and others in Asia, Latin America and central Europe were ready sources of cheap labour and potentially profitable new markets, as their economies expanded. However, globalization has made corporations aware that in these countries there are pools of talented and capable people. It has only been relatively recently (during the last ten years) that businesses have come to understand the potential for skilled labour in parts of the world that they had previously ignored.

People's attitudes are also steadily shifting, one generation at a time. For example, people are accepting more and more that there are no longer 'jobs for life', and anyway increasing numbers of Western employees report that they would not want to stay in the same job throughout their working life. Individuals are likely to have several, even many employers during their career. They are also changing their attitudes to work. Studies by the

Commission of the European Union and the United States Department of Labor have highlighted that people work longer average hours than they used to, and are often prepared to work flexible hours. In return, they expect greater job satisfaction, higher rewards, more personal recognition and a more flexible work environment.

Someone who may come to be seen as a forward-thinking prophet of the new, changing attitudes to employment and leadership is the maverick Ricardo Semler. His company, Semco, was transformed from a struggling machine business, into a profitable, innovative and exciting corporation in a few years, through the aggressive application of employment policies and procedures that actively recognized how work patterns were changing.

Semler holds the view that it is widely accepted that people can participate in local and national democracy, contribute to the community, raise children, express themselves through hobbies and other activities and have the knowledge and potential of the Internet at their fingertips – they are valuable and unique. However, when they go to work they are often treated, en masse, as robots. He therefore set about finding ways to recognize, respect, reward and liberate his workers. For him, the answer was not simply to graft empowerment onto an existing hierarchical structure. Instead, he took a more radical approach with workers empowered (if they want) to find out, discuss and help set the direction of the business, as well as implement it. For example, employees were able to decide the direction of the business, what their targets should be, salary levels and many other issues traditionally left to senior managers. This approach allowed talent throughout the organization to flourish. Furthermore, employees were paid not according to hierarchy or status, but the real value – meaning the scarcity – of what they do. All of this may seem like an impractical socialist utopia but it in fact placed great individual responsibility on Semco's employees, a responsibility that they readily accepted. Individuals were given a much greater say in how their business fared and a much greater control of their fate, and they responded positively as a result.

Semler recognizes the difficulties inherent in this approach. 'At first it was hard for us. But with a great deal of commiseration and consultation the shock of the rulelessness began to subside, and our middle managers began to remove their armour plates. I like to tell them that a turtle may live for hundreds of years because it is well protected by its shell, but it only moves forward when it sticks out its head'.

Interestingly, Semler's views of changing employment patterns extend to his personal life. He sets his priorities for the day and then works to achieve them; once accomplished, he can go home to spend time with his family. Depending on events and how the work progresses, he may finish at lunchtime or midnight, but what he does not do is set a long, interminable list of tasks to accomplish. If managers do this, he believes, they are simply putting undue pressure on themselves, resulting in demotivation, impaired judgement and reduced performance.

Organizations are changing

Competitive pressures for greater flexibility, productivity and cost control are driving changes in the way that organizations are employing people, while social and demographic changes are changing what people want and expect from work. Whereas philosophers such as Karl Marx believed in a fundamental schism between the needs of the employer and those of the worker, in truth, their interests are symbiotic, each needing and valuing the other.

Increasing flexibility requires people to be multi-skilled: not only in the tasks they can accomplish but also the levels at which they work. Consequently, management structures must change to be able to coordinate, respond and learn. It is imperative that bureaucratic organizations change and increase their flexibility. The pressing goal is to focus on *adaptive organizational learning* where sensing and understanding changes in the external environment is routine, and the ability to respond swiftly and effectively is ever-present. Employees must be trained in the skills they will need. Reward systems need to encourage people to take up and apply new skills.

To be more productive, organizations require the right people and the right resources in position at the right time. They must also instill a culture that encourages continuous learning and improvement. This places important, and relatively new, obligations on decision-makers. Among the many factors that help drive productivity, measurement techniques have increasingly been seen as important, hence the popularity from the 1990s of benchmarking, a balanced scorecard approach, and key performance indicators (KPIs). David Norton, co-author of *The Balanced Scorecard* with Robert Kaplan has commented on needing to manage things before you measure them. Professor Donald Marchand, co-author of *Making the Invisible Visible*, takes this view further, in the need to be able to see something before you can measure it and therefore be able to manage it. Professor Marchand's research conducted at IMD business school in Lausanne, Switzerland, is unique in identifying the link between investments in people, information and technology, and bottom line performance. This emphasis on measurement is being embraced by a diverse range of organizations worldwide.

Knowledge matters

It has become evident that what matters in the future is an organization's collective skills and knowledge, and how they are nurtured, managed and developed. This is not to say that knowledge workers providing scarce or unique sources of insight will outnumber other types of employee: rather that the success, and even the survival, of organizations will come to rely more and more on the performance of its knowledge workers. Thomas Stewart, author of *Intellectual Capital* and a prominent writer in this field has commented that: 'Knowledge has become the most important factor in economic life. It is the chief ingredient of what we buy and sell, the raw materials with which we work. Intellectual capital – not natural resources, machinery or even financial capital – has become the one indispensable asset of corporations'. (Reproduced by permission of Nicholas Brealey).

So, what exactly is meant by the term knowledge worker? Management guru Peter Drucker first introduced the term in his 1969 book *The Age of Discontinuity*. Recognizing that the 'corporate man' would not last forever, Drucker perceived the ascendancy of the highly trained, intelligent managerial professional, who understands his own worth and contribution to the organization. Knowledge work is highly specialized and, as a result, can splinter organizations. Consider the range and depth of skills and knowledge needed to manage a chain of retail stores, a hospital, university, automotive manufacturer, pharmaceutical business or high tech company. As the scope and complexity of what we can achieve and what our customers expect deepens, the challenge to keep this expertise coordinated and moving in the right direction becomes greater. The task of employing knowledge in order to achieve this is crucial.

Knowledge is both ownership (by the knowledge worker) and power – a decisive source of competitive advantage. In the words of Lew Platt, former CEO of Hewlett-Packard, 'If H-P knew what it knows, we would be three times as profitable'. Driven by the ability to find, retain and analyse information, resulting from the worldwide growth of technology and the internet, new and decisive sources of competitive advantage have emerged.

Flowing from this is the concept of intellectual capital; this is an asset that is created from knowledge. As Thomas Stewart points out: 'Intelligence becomes an asset when some useful order is created out of free-flowing brainpower... organizational intellect becomes intellectual capital only when it can be deployed to do something that could not be done if it remained scattered round like so many coins in the gutter'. (Reproduced by permission of Nicholas Brealey.) That is another challenge of leadership that was not apparent in previous generations.

A new approach to leadership

Business history is full of the influence of charismatic and visionary people such as Henry Ford, Alfred Sloan, Akio Morita, Harold Geneen, Richard Branson, Jack Welch, Herb Kelleher, Warren Buffett and Bill Gates. But today, charismatic business leaders are less able to influence the business environment. To some extent they can set the agenda, focus and direct, but they are much more vulnerable to the challenges of greater globalization, increasing complexity, the need for innovation and the rising expectations of employees, customers and societies. Charismatic leaders will always inspire but their organizations are likely to succeed only if there are capable, well-organized and imaginative leaders supporting them. That team not only needs to understand their environment – the markets they serve and how they are changing; they also need to use this understanding to inform their personal plans and decisions as well as the way they lead and manage others.

Leadership has many vital elements: for example, getting people engaged and helping them to give their very best; directing their work; empowering them to go further and do more; providing guidance, coaching and developing their team members' skills; building business relationships; getting attitudes and behaviours to change, managing knowledge, information, technology, projects and finance; encouraging teamwork, innovation, decision-making, problem-solving, customer service, and making sure that processes work as well as possible for the benefit of current and potential customers, to name a few. Many of the tasks of leaders depend on the nature of the task they have to complete as well as their specific situation and the people they are leading.

This may seem obvious – possibly even well-worn. After all, leadership has been written about many times, in many different contexts, so what is there new to say? For us, however, considering leadership is a little like examining the sky and the weather. It is ever-present and easy to take for granted, we think we know all there is to know (or at least the most important points) but the truth is we don't: it is unpredictable, brilliant and vital, different in different parts of the world and at varying times, and ever-changing across a range of time horizons.

It is for this reason that one of the vital constituents of an organization that takes talent seriously is that it takes leadership seriously. The two concepts are intertwined and building a talented organization entirely relies on talented leaders.

The business case

The business case for developing talented leaders rests on experience, which suggests that people are ill-equipped to cope with the organizational and business challenges of the twenty-first century. We would call as evidence the period from 1999 to 2009, which included periods of sustained economic growth interspersed with market volatility and punctuated by the biggest global recession since 1945. Business leaders have delivered short-term results but have not demonstrated the personal courage or judgement required to do the right thing consistently in the face of competing stakeholder needs, constant pressure for performance, and the requirement to keep people engaged and motivated at work.

Proving the point that a changing world needs better leadership is the perennially important issue of trust. Let's accept for a moment that life is more complex now than in the 1950s. We can communicate faster and across geographical and time boundaries more easily because of the internet; our purchasing power is greater so we have more choices to make, our attitude to money has changed substantially and social changes (such as less hierarchy, longer working lives, more liberal attitudes) all mean that the opportunities for trust to be relevant in our everyday lives are greater now than before. Also, fewer of us live in homogeneous communities so we have to trust those we don't know and whose backgrounds and culture are not familiar to us.

So, if in 1950 we trusted people or situations 80% of the time and on average we had 10 opportunities a day to decide whether to trust someone or something, then we chose not to trust twice a day. Now, in the twenty-first century, we probably have 100 opportunities a day to decide whether to trust someone or something. We may still trust things 80% of the time, but this means that we are choosing not to trust 20 times a day. These decisions not to trust seem much greater and in real terms, of course, they are, but not in the context of everything else going on around us.

As well as this quantitative argument there is also a qualitative one. Because the frequency of the decisions to trust has increased as the world has become more complex, we have to think about it more and our chances to make the wrong decisions are increased. Even one wrong decision to trust out of 99 correct ones can be disastrous, and that is why trust is so important.

People are the answer (specifically, their head, heart and guts)

So, how can leaders keep pace and succeed in the fast-moving world that we have described? Our search for a solution brings us back to the focus on head, heart and guts described by David L. Dotlich, Peter C. Cairo and Stephen H. Rhinesmith. The difficulty is that leaders often rely exclusively on a single quality: data and rational analysis, emotional connection or courage – but not all three. Concentrating on just one of these dimensions means they ignore other aspects necessary for enduring success. If you rely on your analytical rigour, you may be seen as insensitive or unethical or you may lack the ability to respond outside a narrow range of situations. If you try to create a compassionate culture, you may miss opportunities that a more strategic leader would have seen. Relying solely on the courage of your conviction and toughness may lead you to underestimate the negative consequences for the people you are trying to lead.

Worse than that, taking just one of these approaches to leadership rather than blending and deploying them at the right time has damaging consequences. In particular, leaders intimidate people with their intellect, confuse matters by complicating issues, or dominate conversations. They change direction without being transparent, fail to connect other people's experience to the company's direction, and drive for performance without incorporating other necessary values such as honesty, compassion and trust.

More than ever before, leaders are managing complex situations and constituencies that require a broader range of leadership attributes. They are faced with decisions to which there are no 'right' solutions. They will have to learn how to manage paradoxes rather than try to resolve them. Sometimes they will have to act counter-intuitively and at other times they will need to trust their instincts. Dealing with these difficult and ever-changing situations is not possible without head, heart and guts working together.

Understanding your leadership style

Everyone has a natural leadership style and a tendency to rely on intellect, emotion or courage. While that tend to be fixed, what does change and develop is a willingness to consider options that don't fit with one's natural style, and a capacity for trying new ways of leading others.

Leading for talent requires self-awareness and an understanding of your own style – how you behave and the implications for others around you, both inside and outside the organization. This approach is based on the belief that leadership is situational: you should adjust your style to match each specific challenge. For example, an approach that works well with one group of people may not work well with a different group. Deciding which approach is best involves taking into account: the kind of people you are managing and the type of tasks they are completing.

Understanding different leadership styles

Different styles of leadership are appropriate at different times. The main styles are described below.

Different leadership styles

Leadership style	Characteristics
Directing (telling) This involves: structure; control and supervision; one way communication	This approach is effective when the team is new, temporary or forming. The leader is hands-on, decisive and involved with the needs of the task and the team. They direct the team and stress the importance of tasks and deadlines.
Coaching (engaging) This involves: directing and supporting; teaching skills	This style is often preferred when the team has worked together for some time and has developed understanding and expertise. It works when a balance is needed between short- and long-term aspects. The leader needs to monitor the achievement of targets, but longer-term elements, such as communication networks and decision-making processes, are also important.
Supporting (developing) This involves: praising, listening and facilitating development	This is suitable for a situation in which a team continues to function well. The leader has empowered their staff and is no longer involved in short-term performance and operational measures. Also, the longer-term is significant, with the leader focusing on individual and team development, planning and innovation.

Leadership style	Characteristics
Delegating ('hands-off' facilitation) This involves: turning over responsibility for routine decisions	This is a 'hands-off' style that works best with a highly-experienced, successful team. The team works well with very little involvement from the leader; instead, the leadership role is often to work externally for the team, developing networks, gaining resources, sharing best practice and expertise. Leaders may intervene in the team, if requested, to help define problems and devise solutions or if a problem arises.

Success as a leader relies on using the right style at the right time. Such situational leadership draws on four management styles: directing, coaching, supporting and delegating. Adapt your approach to suit each situation.

Each style is effective at different times. A directional approach is most appropriate when the leader needs to tell people what to do, perhaps in a crisis or when dealing with difficult personnel issues. This should be used only in exceptional circumstances. Delegating, supporting and coaching styles can be seen as a democratic approach, with the leader seeking consensus and engaging the team. This works best when you need to get your team to commit to a course of action.

To develop your leadership style, it is necessary to understand the impact of your behaviour and then to adjust your style to ensure successful leadership. There are many ways to explore this, from coaching to psychometric tests or 360-degree appraisals.

More straightforwardly, ask you team to answer three questions:

• What do I do well?
• What's missing for you?
• What do I need to work on?

You may be surprised by their answers. This moves away from the old hierarchy that as a leader you need to know all the answers. It also shifts the power relationship between you and your colleagues onto a more equal footing. This type of leadership calls for an approach more akin to the conductor than the general. We realize that this will be challenging particularly if you have always seen yourself as the 'boss' and have enjoyed the authority this commands. Take time to reflect on what's driving your need to be 'in charge' and examine the benefits in leading a team that think and act more autonomously.

In our experience when people become conscious of their development in these areas they often think can concentrate on fixing their weaker areas rather than playing to their strengths. Good leaders are aware of their weaknesses and take steps to minimise these. Exceptional leaders however, play to their strengths and create a distinctive leadership signature. They know when and how to apply their abilities and are consciously aware of not overplaying them. Being brilliant at analysis, for example, is out of place when action is required. The key here is to focus on becoming a more complete, agile leader and take time to consciously reflect on how your behaviour affects those around you.

Finally, your personal style and behaviours are based on your core beliefs and sense of purpose. These are set at the heart of who you are and it is worth reflecting on how these became important to you and if they are still relevant to who you are today.

Taking leadership seriously

Today, many companies still develop their leaders the way they did when leadership demands were different. For example, they often use traditional classroom training, focusing almost exclusively on cognitive learning. Even when more effective and imaginative methods are used (such as project work or temporary assignments) the danger is that people revert to their old way of doing things when they return to the workplace. To develop capable leaders, however, organizations need to move away from this traditional approach and instead embrace a more holistic way of working.

Global challenges such as negotiating, making decisions and communicating require leaders to integrate and display brains, emotional intelligence and courage. Unfortunately, leadership development programmes fail to help people learn how to integrate the three elements. Hiring, rewards and recognition processes also usually emphasize the importance of managerial competence.

And, as we have previously stated the game has changed; priority must be given to how everyone delivers value and the leader's task is to deliver this to the organization and its shareholders – not simply moving resources from A to B.

A systemic approach means moving away from an over reliance on class-room based leadership education and looking at a series of activities which touch on each element of your organization's talent ecology.

1. Revisit the business strategy and be clear about the capabilities required in the short, medium and long term.

2. Build a comprehensive picture of the external forces affecting the performance of the business. Talk to customers and stalk competitors! It's striking how introspective we can get when as leaders we are busy getting the job done. We once witnessed a room full of bank managers fall silent when asked to name the interest rate on the mortgage product of a competitor further down the high street. From a cus-tomer perspective it is essential that you understand how people experience your brand, product, service or campaign. How easy was it to buy from you? Did the product deliver? Will you come back and recommend? These questions are not the sole domain of the marketing department. They provide vital insights into how well your organization is working, the capabilities required for leaders and the workforce as a whole.

    Different combinations of head, heart and guts are needed in different situations. Also, as people move through different levels in an organization, they must adjust their behaviours and values accordingly.

3. Be aware of the systemic issues that will influence how people engage with the learning activity and how they apply the learning back in the workplace. This means articulating potential obstacles, such as a risk-averse company culture, that make it difficult for leaders to show heart and guts behaviours or to think in ways that may run counter to the

culture. This is a critical process that is often neglected. The need is clear: what is the point of encouraging a leader to think and behave differently, flexibly and in such a way that they can meet the fast-moving challenges they encounter, only for their bosses to then expect them to operate in the same historic way as before?

4. **Involve the executive committee.** This links closely with the previous point: for leadership to succeed it needs to run consistently through the organization and everyone needs to understand and embrace the need for a head, heart and guts approach. Involvement isn't just about review and sign off. Senior leaders need to be engaged in the detail and understand the implications for the organization. Our experience is that they are more than keen to do this but given their workloads need a clear business case (qualitative and quantitative) together with dedicated time to shape the agenda. Alongside this we recommend that the whole team is engaged and that they nominate a need to go on and sponsor the project.

5. **Teach your leaders how to be teachers.** Good leaders have huge influence on how talent develops. Often however this is more about luck than judgement and the people who do it well will tell you that it is just 'something I've always done'. It is striking that increasingly the tools for good talent development are located in the HR department or outsourced to consultancies. We recommend underlining the importance of this by introducing techniques into induction/orientation and highlighting role model behaviour in performance conversations.

6. On the subject of induction and orientation of new leaders it is also striking to reflect on how rarely this happens well. As we point out in the Talent Doom Loop some companies estimate that up to 25% of new senior hires leave after their first year. And, it is rare that those achieving promotions within the organization receive dedicated support to make their transition effective. These are two crucial moments in an employee's experience of your employee value proposition. They will make or break their future effectiveness and the degree to which they share their potential with you.

7. **Use leadership development as a business improvement tool.** Individuals that are developing their leadership skills can make top

management aware of systemic issues by providing honest, incisive feedback.

8. Remember to build diversity into the overall approach. This means being clear about the core leadership capabilities required for your strategy and the range of different styles required to exercise them. Context is key and it is important to educate leaders on when and how they might flex their styles. In terms of people diversity, review who is making it through to leadership positions and how promotions happen. How well does your leadership population reflect your desired customer base? What might be getting in the way of minority groups progressing?

9. Customize the development activity for your organization, incorporating head, heart and guts. This takes in to account the specific culture and situation and ensures that the three attributes are developed in a way that is mutually-reinforcing. Be realistic about the anticipated learning outcomes; stick to the ones that will really make a difference and remember that every person will have an individual approach to this so ensure that there is space for individuals to explore their personal development needs. Think about using blended learning tools (e.g. action learning, mentoring, pod-casts and projects work) to enable employees to customize the learning experience. It is also worth remembering that the most effective vehicle for learning is actually teaching, so consider involving role model leaders in development activity; in our experience technical experts enjoy taking a thought leadership role and senior executives willingly sponsor project based activity and mentoring.

10. Ensure that culture and process work to reinforce the need to take leadership seriously. How are people rewarded and recognized? Is recruitment and promotion based on robust criteria? Are leaders accredited to lead others? How often do the Board review the quality of the organization's leaders?

Organizations must help leaders build their capacity to exhibit head, heart and guts as complete leaders at the right times in the right situations. We believe that this approach to leading and engaging talent will provide an invaluable, thought-provoking way for leaders who want to move beyond their leadership comfort zone and meet the challenges of twenty-first century leadership.

Developing a systemic, integrated approach is what the organization needs to do, but what are the priorities for the individual? What should you do if you want to succeed as a twenty-first-century leader? Brains, emotional intelligence and courage combine, together providing a vital focus for a wide range of skills and techniques. These are explained further in the next chapter.

Leadership reflections

When reviewing how well you lead for talent:

- Reflect on previous situations and on things people have told you, to understand how you typically behave.
- Ask others how they view your style.
- Decide if you move easily from one style to another, as appropriate, or whether you have one dominant style.
- Seek feedback from a wide range of people; your line manager, your peers and your direct reports. Some 360 feedback tools now extend to include friends and family who are well-placed to comment on differences in your style between work at home.
- Critically examine what people tell you with specific questions. For example: Is your personal style overly formal, informal or balanced? Does it encourage and empower people? Is it prescriptive or controlling? What effect are you having on others – why might this be and how could it improve or develop?
- Take time to understand your strengths and the qualities that make you distinctive. Imagine the style in your leadership signature, does it accurately reflect your sense of personal purpose? Will it engage others enough to work with you?
- When you are at your best do you lead through your head, heart or guts? In what instances might you have overplayed your style and how might you adapt this to different circumstances?

- Are you clear about your own sense of purpose and career path? To what extent do your underlying beliefs influence your behaviour in different situations? Are you willing to take risks in ambiguous situations? Do you feel confident in making decisions with limited information? How interested are you in the personal motivations and aspirations of those you work with? How willing are you to give up traditional notions of status?

In many ways, courage can be learned and people can overcome their fears and learn to take risks if they are conscious of and practise behaviours associated with five traits: purpose, will, rigour, risk and candour. Leaders don't have to show courage all the time – they simply need to know when and how to display it during defining moments.

- Consider how your beliefs on what talent looks like have been shaped? They are likely to have been influenced by those you have worked with before, where you worked and the particular code of success in different organizations. Do you have an inclusive or exclusive idea of what talent is? How relevant are these to your current organization, will they complement the strategy and drive the business forward?

- How well do you understand the psychology of human development, motivation and adult learning? What new techniques could you experiment with to further build the capability of your team?

Chapter 10

Techniques for Realizing Talent in Your Whole Workforce

Michelangelo is often quoted as having said that inside every block of stone or marble dwells a beautiful statue: one needs only to remove the excess material to reveal the work of art within. If we are to apply this visionary concept to education, it would be pointless to compare one child to another. Instead, all the energy would be focused on chipping away at the stone, getting rid of whatever is in the way of each child's developing skills, mastery and self-expression.

We call this practice 'giving an A'. An A can be given to anyone in any walk of life. When you give an A you find yourself speaking to people not from a place of measuring how they stack up against your standards, but from a place of respect that gives them room to realize themselves. Your eye is on the statue within the roughness of the uncut stone.

Rosamund Stone Zander, Benjamin Zander, *The Art of Possibility*
(Harvard Business School Press, 2000 p. 26)

As we saw in the previous chapter, the twentieth century was a period of great economic, technological and social change. Many of these changes are clear, obvious and understood, but some of them are less perceptible, perhaps because they have taken place over longer timescales. For example, in the 1990s, several important developments started affecting the way that people are employed. First, globalization began to bring people and whole societies into the world economy in a way that had not been seen before. Second, technology has been profoundly changing the way we work: what we do and how we do it. In the view of Bill Emmott, a former editor of *The*

Economist: 'The impact of new technology is almost always over-estimated in the short-term and under-estimated in the long-term'. Third, organizations increasingly outsource activities relating to managing people. Fourth, organizations rely more on people who are neither full-time nor permanent employees. Fifth, knowledge is recognized as being important in a way that hasn't really happened before. And finally, linking these points together is the fact that people are increasingly seen not just as employees but as valuable contributors to an organization's success. Their ability is an asset and their potential is essential to sustainable growth.

As we have discussed in chapter 8, great leaders need to be able to balance intellect, emotional intelligence and courage – qualities referred to by business writers David L. Dotlich, Peter C. Cairo and Stephen H. Rhinesmith in their book *Head, Heart and Guts: How the world's best companies develop complete leaders* (Jossey-Bass, 2006). So, how can you ensure that as a leader you use all three attributes, in the right way and at the right time?

This chapter explores the vital links between leadership and talent and answers several questions: how do you attract good people to your organization and how can you ensure that they achieve their full potential? How do you stimulate, engage and inspire people at all levels to achieve greatness? What practical support do people really want at work and what do they get? Above all, how can you build a dynamic workforce, help people realize their potential and enable them to succeed?

In fact, being able to engage talent requires great insight and skill. When it comes to the relationship between work, leadership and business success, the links are complicated but undeniable and hugely significant.

Leading with your heart

How do you lead with your heart? What does it mean and what, in practice, does it involve? The answer is simple: the key is to bring feelings and emotions to bear on business decisions, in a way that is profitable and sustainable. Many leaders believe that the most important motivator for people is compensation. Studies of employee attitudes show, however, that what is really important to people is the quality of their work environment, how they are treated by their boss, and whether their work is meaningful and contributes to the organization's success. After all, it is often said that people join an organization but they leave a manager. Several steps are significant when leading with your heart.

Balance the needs of individuals and the business

Clearly, there is an increasing pressure on leaders to deliver improved performance, but while a 'heartless', single-minded focus on results may meet short-term business requirements, it will erode company morale, increase employee turnover and fail to gain true commitment to the business. The ability to foster inclusiveness and be empathetic can have a dramatic impact on performance, especially in the long term.

To develop greater empathy and to better understand the emotions of others, get in the habit of asking people for their views and then exploring these. Also, reflect on how and why they are saying something – and what they are not saying. Finally, think about how someone might feel by thinking how you would feel in the same situation.

Know yourself and connect emotionally to others

The concept of emotional intelligence makes a big difference in an individual's ability to lead and influence. The benefits of maintaining a balance between people and results are long-term sustainability, innovation (people are not afraid to challenge conventional ways of doing things), and more networking and connectivity between groups to get things done.

Developing self-awareness is an important, perennial leadership quality and a vital place to start. Succeeding at work and building your career require self-awareness and an understanding of your own style: how you behave and the implications for others around you, both inside and outside your organization. People who are self-aware:

- Know how they feel and how they are likely to react.
- Understand the advantages and potential pitfalls of passion and emotion.
- Recognize and develop their strengths and look for opportunities to excel.

- Display emotional intelligence – they are sensitive to others' feelings and have the ability to influence people.

The first step is to pay attention to emotions – yours and others'. Despite the fact that our moods run alongside our thoughts, we rarely pay much attention to the way we feel. This is significant because previous emotional experiences provide a context for our decisions. Being aware of one's feelings, and able to manage these feelings, is essential, as it affects issues such as control, personal development, confidence and self-belief.

To increase self-awareness, ask yourself when, why and how you do something. For example: When do you get most upset? Why do you dislike something? How do you typically react?

Stay self-aware

Self-awareness is vital for managers. If you aren't self-aware, or if you haven't attended to your own development as a coach, then it's more likely that you'll find yourself either in a rut, uncertain or out of options. The first principle, therefore, is to stay aware and attend to your professional development.

Studies such as those by Malcolm Higgs and Victor Dulewicz at Henley Business School* have found that the most statistically significant factors contributing to career success (as measured by increases in job position and salary) are *self-awareness* and *emotional resilience*. Certainly, the best way to help people to develop their self-awareness and emotional resilience, two longstanding and widely-recognized attributes of great leaders, is to include coaching alongside other development activities, such as 360-degree feedback and experiential development. For example, psychometric tests such as the classic Myers-Briggs Type Indicator (MBTI) are invaluable for developing self-awareness. MBTI's value lies in helping people understand how they and others perceive the world and make decisions.

---

* For further information see *Making Sense of Emotional Intelligence* by Malcolm Higgs and Victor Dulewicz, published by National Foundation for Educational Research.

Develop empathy

Closely linked to self-awareness is the ability to understand, and adjust to, emotions in others. This matters because it results in greater insight, understanding and, crucially, influence. Empathy leads to greater influence. It is the way to persuade others to change, as your ideas are based on an understanding of their position and the need to provide a reason for change.

Empathizing means understanding the other person's situation. This is most obviously achieved by putting yourself in the other person's position. This will help to understand and overcome their concerns and keep their commitment to you and the task at hand. Empathy also means 'speaking their language' and getting your message across in terms they will respond to and clearly understand.

There are many ways to develop and display empathy and while some people find it easy, for others it can be a challenge. Techniques that can help include developing your knowledge and use of body language. Understanding non-verbal communication is a valuable way to uncover how people feel as well as what they think about an issue. Also, prepare to empathize by considering – in advance of a meeting, negotiation or discussion – how you might react or behave in the specific situation. Consider what is reasonable and what motivations would drive possible reactions. Find out about different causes of motivation.

Other techniques include seeking specific feedback – the more specific the feedback you obtain the easier it will be for you to track progress and develop this skill. Also, focus on what people are really saying, not what you think they are saying, and 'speak their language' so that you get your message across in terms that others will respond to and understand.

Other techniques that help build empathy include *questioning*, a vital way to improve understanding, test assumptions and show that you are listening. This can also involve summarizing key points in the conversation so as to prevent misunderstandings and move the conversation on to the next point.

When developing empathy it is essential to maintain professionalism and control your emotions by being critically aware. For example: react to ideas, not people, by focusing on the significance to the discussion of the facts and evidence and listening for how things are said (and what is not said). Also, avoid taking quick decisions – instead, give yourself time to think and react; remember to recognize your own views and biases, and be sensitive and tactful, especially when disagreeing or questioning. Choose your words carefully.

Remain in control
Self-regulation is the ability to understand and manage your feelings. It is the reason why self-awareness is so valuable and it is fundamental to succeeding at work. People who are in control and self-regulate:

- recall their past successes, as a way of boosting confidence;
- remain fully focused on the task in hand;
- understand their impact on others;
- recognize their own limitations;
- analyse their own reactions;
- find time to renew their energy;
- possess clear standards and values.

To improve self-regulation, it can help to consider what situations cause stress, frustration, disappointment or other negative emotions. Also, what helps you to feel confident, in control, energetic, creative or any other positive feelings; how do you approach conflicts and problems, and how this might improve?

Use different styles of working
A person's approach to work is situational. This means you should adjust your style to match each specific challenge or situation. For example, an approach that works well with one group of people may not work well with a different group. To decide which approach is best, think about: the kind of people you are working with and the type of tasks that are being completed.

Being successful with leadership styles relies on using the right style at the right time. Also, when working with a member of your team, the question to consider is whether to focus on their skills (their competence) or their attitude (commitment). Finally, each style is effective at different times. To know which style is appropriate, look at how effectively someone is working.

To improve your self-awareness, consider several key questions (these are also a valuable way for coaches to develop greater self-awareness in others):

Many leaders believe that the most important motivator for people is compensation. Studies of employee attitudes show, however, that what is really important to people is the quality of their work environment, how they are treated by their boss, and whether their work is meaningful and contributes to the organization's success.

- What are your strengths – the things you really excel at?
- What do you enjoy and want to improve?
- What are your weaknesses – where would it help you to improve and how will you do this?
- When, how often and how effectively do you analyse your strengths and weaknesses?
- Do you play to your strengths and manage your weaknesses?
- Are you aware of your limitations?
- Do you understand your true potential and do you have a plan for achieving it?
- Do you recognize when you need a break?
- Do you manage your emotions successfully and do you recognize emotion in others?
- Do you delegate when you know that other people will get a better result?
- What causes you stress and what gives you energy?
- Do you understand how your behaviour can affect others?
- What is your potential – what would you like to achieve in the future?

Coaching and other methods of leadership development are also valuable, because they enable a leader to acknowledge the reality of competing needs that must be balanced. Coaching helps leaders stay in touch with their own heart and emotions, and change from driving to listening modes – something that is difficult for most strong leaders.

Develop emotional intelligence (EQ)

'Emotional intelligence' is a person's ability to acquire and apply knowledge from their emotions and the emotions of others, so they can be more successful and lead a more fulfilling life. Its value lies in enabling us to sense and use emotions, helping us to manage ourselves and build positive, productive relationships.

Psychologist Daniel Goleman popularized his view of emotional intelligence in the 1995 best-seller *Emotional Intelligence: Why it can matter more than IQ.* Building on the work of Howard Gardner and Peter Salovey he highlighted the fact that emotions are critical in determining a leader's success. In times of change, pressure or crisis, possessing emotional intelligence is an advantage as success is determined by recognizing, understanding and dealing with emotions. For example, we may all feel anger but emotional intelligence means knowing what to do with the emotion of anger to achieve the best outcome.

Emotional Intelligence is evident in five areas:

- knowing one's emotions;
- managing emotions;
- motivating people;
- recognizing emotions in others;
- handling relationships.

These 'emotional competencies' build on each other in a hierarchy. At the bottom of his hierarchy ('1') is the ability to identify one's emotional state. Some knowledge of competency 1 is needed to move to the next competency. Likewise, knowledge or skill in the first three competencies is needed to show empathy, reading and influencing positively other people's emotions (competency 4). The first four competencies lead to increased ability to enter and sustain good relationships (competency 5).

Inspire trust

What are the basic laws of engendering trust? What do trusted individuals do, and what do they avoid doing? It is useful to remember several important points. First, self-trust is a vital factor in creating trust – if you don't trust yourself, it is unlikely that others will. Also, trust is an absolute, there is no such thing as partial trust, it is an 'either/or'. Either it exists or it does not. We either trust someone or we do not.

People who are trusted enjoy great insight into their own patterns of behaviour and motivation. They can answer questions such as 'Why do I behave the way I do?' 'What motivates me?' 'What affects my behaviour?' Understanding these questions will enable you to deliver the core requirements of trust, such as fairness, openness, courage and the other drivers of trust. This personal insight is, of course, notoriously difficult to achieve, and many people make a great deal of money helping to find the answers.

Leaders need to find the right balance between control and trust. Trust is not a coat, a temporary 'quick fix' approach that we can use when it suits us and discard when we choose. It is a genuine belief system. We don't trust people for our own personal gain. We trust them because it is the right thing to do, and, in the end, we all benefit by doing the right thing.

Trust is vital for creating a positive culture of engagement and commitment. It is fundamental to such issues as sharing knowledge, generating innovative ideas, building customer loyalty, winning new business, motivating people and leading change. Without trust, all of these issues become much, much harder to achieve.

Yet inspiring trust should not be a difficult issue, it simply requires us to be confident, open, consistent, honest and dynamic. In particular, it means doing what you say you will and setting an example for others to follow. Interestingly, recent scientific research by Nobel laureate Vernon Smith and others has highlighted the fact that people tend to reciprocate naturally and instinctively when they are trusted. If you trust someone, they are much more likely to trust you.

Inspiring trust means leading from the front, setting and demonstrating the standards for integrity, trust, personal values, initiative, dynamism and teamwork that others can follow. Trust also requires leaders to encourage and motivate people. If your colleagues are to use their initiative and energies to take the business forward and embrace change, then a positive, open and blame-free environment is an important prerequisite. Finally, inspiring trust is essential for focusing, engaging and directing people so that they realize their potential, focus on customer issues and adapt positively to change. In fact, trust is so significant that it is worth emphasizing the nature of trust and why it matters.

First, trust makes it easier for things to change. Trusted leadership is essential for meeting the challenges of changing conditions. People need to be able to rely on each other when everything else may be shifting. People who enjoy the support of others are more likely to do things differently, better, and take measured risks than people who are concerned, alone and disinclined to trust.

Also, trust matters because it is a common currency, universally understood and valued. Although the context in which trust exists may vary, from a personal connection to an organization's relationship with millions of customers, or from a factory in Cleveland to a bank in Shanghai, everyone understands what trust is and why it is important. In adversity, people look for trust and, when they find it, they value and treasure it. Also, what is frequently overlooked is the corollary of trust being welcomed: an absence of trust does not result in a neutral situation. It invariably means something much, much worse. When trust is lost, there is a high cost to pay.

In addition, people respond better to people who they trust than to people they don't. This matters if you are trying to achieve anything: motivate someone, sell to a customer, share ideas, maximize opportunities or prevent or solve a problem – the list is endless.

Trust also matters because formal rules will never be enough. The spirit of an agreement, a positive desire to work in good faith to achieve desired outcomes, is often as important to success as the letter of the law. Given mankind's immense ingenuity there may always be ways of circumventing formal rules, so they should not be relied on in isolation. After all, even the most basic laws only succeed because they have the support of the people.

Quite apart from their intrinsic moral benefits, trust and integrity are the most easily defended virtues. People understand that honesty is the best policy and respect those that demonstrate this virtue. Customers and colleagues alike value trust; they are much more likely to engage with you in a way that benefits you and your business. Put another way, dishonesty will probably lead to difficult decisions becoming worse and future decisions may prove impossible, as people's trust and respect will haemorrhage should they encounter manipulation or deceit. However, honesty in decision-making does not mean being insensitive, it simply means doing the right thing. At times, this can call for tact, sensitivity and understanding; all of these are preferable to dishonesty and other unethical behaviours that are counter-productive and damaging.

Interesting research* about the issue of trust asked people to rate the significance of a wide range of attributes when deciding whether to trust someone. The top ten most popular attributes were found to be:

1. Fairness.
2. Dependability.
3. Respect.
4. Openness.
5. Courage.
6. Unselfishness.
7. Competence.
8. Supportiveness.
9. Empathy.
10. Compassion.

These are *the drivers of trust*. Understanding and delivering each of these qualities is vital if trust is to be developed. These attributes are typically what we look for when deciding whether to trust and, quite probably, how much to trust someone. However, the reality of trust, meaning the attributes that we normally find, is quite different from this list. When people were asked which attributes were most frequently encountered it produced the following results:

*For further information see *A Question of Trust* by Sally Bibb and Jeremy Kourdi, published by Marshall Cavendish.

1.   Likeability.
2.   Dependability.
3.   Criticalness.
4.   Ambition.
5.   Fairness
6.   Professionalism.
7.   Competence.
8.   Respect.
9.   Controllingness.
10. Predictability.

These attributes are *the reality of trust*. Interestingly, only four of the drivers of trust were in the top ten most commonly found attributes: fairness, dependability, respect and competence. Meaning there are six attributes that we value significantly that are relatively scarce: openness, courage, unselfishness, supportiveness, empathy and compassion.

The research then looked a little deeper and identified those attributes where what we find in reality falls short of what we look for – our ideal. We call this variance between what we look for and what we find *the trust deficit* – a gap in our expectations. The attributes with the biggest gap between what we want and what we find are:

1.   Courage.
2.   Unselfishness.
3.   Fairness.
4.   Openness.
5.   Compassion.
6.   Respect.
7.   Dependability.
8.   Empathy.
9.   Vision.
10. Supportiveness.

To develop trust we should understand what these attributes mean for the way we relate to people. Not only are these the qualities that we typically look for when deciding whether to trust someone, they are also the qualities where our expectations are most seriously missed.

Trust is recognized as being fragile and tricky to build, so it should come as no surprise if this list appears demanding – perhaps even daunting. To succeed, it is worth taking the time to consider each attribute in turn.

Be courageous. This means different things to different people but above all, it implies an ability to do and say what you mean, especially when faced with adversity. It also requires a capacity to take risks, to be constant and determined, to admit mistakes and to stand alone when necessary. The value of courage is that it is universally respected. Even if we do not agree with a particular idea or approach, we admire bravery and associated qualities of integrity, conviction and determination. Moral courage – the courage of our convictions – is present in those people that we choose to trust.

Behave unselfishly. One of the biggest counters to trust is a feeling that people are motivated by narrow self-interest, that life (and particularly commerce) is a zero sum game. If this view predominates then logic dictates that the only sensible course of action is to always put oneself first. However, there are two problems with this view. First, life is not simply a zero sum game with winners and losers – it is much more complex (and interesting). Second, even if it was a zero sum game – there are occasions when someone must 'win' at another's expense – behaving selfishly is not always the answer.

Value fairness. The next attribute we look for when deciding to trust is fairness. People that are most often and most easily trusted behave fairly. This means that they treat others:

- according to what is understood and accepted to be reasonable;
- as they would wish to be treated themselves;
- in a consistent, even-handed manner.

Being fair does not simply mean avoiding inequity and preventing unfairness; rather, it implies a dynamic, proactive desire to seek out what is just, and then follow that course. In this respect, fairness links closely with the need to be courageous, unselfish, open, empathic, compassionate and consistent.

Openness engages people – and for organizations, this includes customers as well as employees, suppliers and others.

Be open. Openness is most frequently discussed in relation to corporate governance issues but it is no less important in the appearance and feeling one gives to others. Are you approachable? Do people feel inclined to come and talk to you?

Openness matters because people that shift their viewpoints, or are genuinely unclear about an issue, are not easily trusted. Openness is therefore linked with one essential quality: self-awareness. This may seem counterintuitive when it comes to the issue of trust, which is focused on other people and relationships. However, being self-aware is an important and frequently neglected issue. So, how can we develop and sustain openness and generate greater trust?

- *Engage people* by involving individuals in decisions, inviting and respecting their contribution and encouraging them to challenge each other.
- *Be self-aware.* You may *think* that you are open to other people's ideas, perceptions and behaviours but do others perceive you as genuinely open?
- *Provide clarity and explain.* This is also important for openness and trust. It reassures people that their opinions have been considered and opens people up to the reasoning and intention behind a decision.

Develop empathy, compassion and supportiveness. Although these are different attributes they are closely related in the ways they contribute to trust. Empathy is defined as the ability to understand and enter into another person's feelings, while compassion recognizes the need to do something about the situation we find. The reason that people who display empathy and compassion are trusted is because they give others a genuine feeling that their feelings and circumstances are being considered and understood. In other words, there is more at play than simply the leader's own self-interest.

Give respect and credit to others. Trust is likely to result when people are clearly shown respect, because respect is seen as a clear, positive and engaging virtue. At times, showing respect can also be disarming and this, too, is positive for generating trust. Many people and organizations are trusted because they are respected. They have shared values and these provide a common language that brings people closer together. Trust occurs because people feel that these individuals and firms are on their 'wavelength', valuing what they value, seeing the world in a similar way and giving things the same relative value they do. This concept of *congruency* is a central pillar of trust and respect.

Crucially, respect is not just about friendship or feeling good – it is much more about wanting and feeling able to do the things that count. Leadership at any level is full of tough decisions; the way these are resolved has major consequences for the level of respect that is accorded to them.

There are many personal perspectives on building respect; however, respected people – like respected organizations – invariably possess some or all of the following characteristics:

- They know what it is that they have to achieve, possessing clarity of vision and purpose.
- They are interested in what they do, displaying energy and enthusiasm at all levels.
- They understand and accept the expectations that are held about them.
- They challenge and propose new ways of doing things, searching for new ideas.
- They feel they have the authority to take decisions, and exercise this authority responsibly.
- They are supportive, with an emotional attachment to colleagues and an expectation of reciprocal respect and support.

Be dependable. Dependability develops trust. This is because cooperation and collaboration are often integral to dependability, with people encouraged to support each other with practical help, good communication and in other ways – from mentoring to sharing best practice and experience. Dependability also has something in common with the other attributes of trust, such as courage, unselfishness, fairness and compassion. Like them, it can mean giving up things – information, time, resources, pet projects – to help others succeed. To illustrate the impact of dependability, consider the three most trustworthy people you have ever met and ask: how dependable are they?

Being dependable simply means being reliable and consistent. It enables people to know what to expect and it facilitates communication and collaboration, as well as providing the certainty needed to encourage and motivate.

Show visionary thinking. If people are to place their trust in someone, they need to know where they are heading and they need to be motivated to make the journey. If they are uncertain or lack the necessary motivation, then trust will be eroded. The value of visionary leadership, therefore, is that it provides a clear direction or set of values – and it motivates. Being visionary means encouraging people to look at activities in the long-term, keeping in mind overall goals. The orientation is to the future, seeing things in the broadest context and appreciating broad principles. In a stronger form, it involves inspiring others with the goals to be achieved.

The characteristics of a compelling vision that generates trust include:

- Realism – it must comprize feasible, attainable goals.
- Power – this has two parts: it must be *imaginable* and paint a clear picture of what the future will look like; it must also *excite and inspire* as many people as possible.
- Communicability – it must be possible for the vision to be communicated to anyone, *quickly* and *easily*.
- Desirability – the vision needs to appeal to the long-term interests of all the stakeholders. These chiefly include customers, employees and shareholders.
- Focus – the vision needs to be specific and 'real-world' enough to be used as a basis for strategic planning and to provide guidance for decision-making.

- Adaptability – the vision needs to allow individual initiative in how it is attained and flexible enough to allow for changing conditions.

Focus on intentions. Our intentions matter – both the ends we seek and the means we use. This is essential if trust is to be developed, but what else is needed for it to take hold and thrive? How should we behave if we want to create trust? Definitions of trust vary, but research into the issue has highlighted that many people perceive trust as meaning two different but related things: predicting how someone else will behave, and also expecting someone to do what is best for you. It is therefore worth considering:

- What trust means to you – where, when and why it matters.
- Who do you respect and trust – what is it about them that engenders trust?
- How could trust benefit your organization? In what areas would greater trust improve performance, for example, building your brand, strengthening customer loyalty, lowering recruitment costs, increasing innovation, enhancing leadership and productivity?
- How much does your organization lose because trust is weak or missing?

There are several other useful questions that can help focus your thinking about trust.

Find ways to resolve issues and provide support. Collaboration develops trust and this can be achieved by:

- Establishing regular opportunities for colleagues to meet informally.
- Allowing time at team meetings for an open exchange of views: look for what people think as well as what they say.
- Establishing a project team with complementary skills, drawing on people who do not usually collaborate, and get them to work on a specific issue or challenge.
- Confronting poor performance. If people are behaving ineffectively and are unaware that their actions are causing concern, tell them (preferably in confidence).

Build a strong team. This is a vital leadership role: it not only inspires trust but encourages others to trust each other and it ensures that the talents of the team are allowed to flow. Team building can be enhanced by:

- Keeping team members informed.
- Giving constructive feedback.
- Recognizing success.
- Finding ways to build relationships.
- Being honest and open.

Be decisive. Do not simply hope that trust will emerge as people get to know you. It might, but that is not going to be enough in high pressure or high-risk situations. More likely, you will need to take charge, deciding what outcome you want and how best to achieve it. This might mean no more than setting a time limit and monitoring a situation or it could mean getting much more involved and mediating.

Use the trust cycle. Building trust can be accomplished by repeating each of the following stages in the trust cycle, in sequence. Missing one stage takes you back to the start, and makes it harder to build trust in the future. This approach can be taken with team members or clients – wherever trust needs to be built.

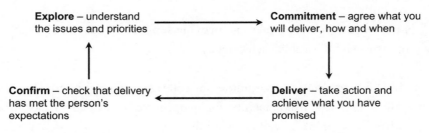

The Trust Cycle

Avoid becoming emotional, stressed or losing objectivity. Cynicism, tiredness, frustration, impatience, criticism and other negative behaviours are to be avoided, as they frustrate the free flow of ideas and jeopardize the trust that people have in you. It can be easy to get drawn into a conflict or manipulated into taking sides. You should be aware of the pitfalls and decide early on how you will approach the dispute. The first step when dealing with anxiety is to remember that it is a natural state that exists any time we are placed under stress.

To help you deal with stressful situations, take some time to identify the types of situations that make you feel stressful. For example some people find public speaking quite stressful. For each situation, list what it is that actually makes you anxious. Write down the worst thing that could happen. Many fears do not look frightening at all once you confront them. Now think about what you can do to cope with the stressful situation. Take time to organize what you require, visualize your success and, if appropriate, practice being successful before the situation occurs.

Respond to ideas and develop a positive mindset. People are more likely to trust you and share their thoughts, fears and ideas if they believe that they will be received enthusiastically and with respect. This can mean being positive – looking on the bright side and seeking the best from an idea, action or comment. It may also mean exploring several ideas fully before deciding which to support, identifying the benefits of change and the new idea, and then actively selling them and building on ideas constructively.

Sometimes people react to stress with negative criticism and hence talk themselves into failure. To increase your positive mindset don't try to be a perfectionist – many people increase their stress by trying to deliver an exceptional outcome, when an acceptable one is sufficient. You need to determine when it is necessary to deliver a perfect outcome and when you need to let go. Avoid personalizing all outcomes, as this will under-mine your mindset. What was within your control? What was outside of your control? When you personalize outcomes, seeing yourself as the cause of a negative outcome that is outside of your control, you increase your stress and frustration. Finally, talk positively and emphasize the positive. Identify what you did well, not just what you didn't do well. Congratulate yourself on your successes. Think optimistically – imagine the best, rather than the worst.

Invite feedback. Inviting feedback is a great way of showing openness and trust in others, and inspiring trust in return. Feedback is useful, and inviting it involves targeting specific people to get feedback from, being specific about what you want comments on and being open about why. It is particularly important to avoid becoming defensive or arguing with the comments; instead, reflect on it carefully and decide whether to act. Finally, understand that it may be difficult for people to give feedback, so be sensitive and thank them.

Increase collaboration. Collaboration can help to increase employee engagement. Collaboration is strengthened if people have:

- Shared values and a shared vision.
- A single identity and focus.
- Frequent communication.
- Empowerment, with people working on their own initiative.
- Courtesy and respect.

The same issue can be viewed from the opposite perspective: what are the factors that typically frustrate or reduce collaboration? Important issues are:

- Intra-company rivalry.
- Personalities and individual agendas.
- Recognition and rewards focused on individuals – rather than on collective behaviour.
- Business planning takes place largely in business 'silos'. This contributes to conflicting interests.
- Poor communication and a lack of a shared vision.

Several techniques can help you develop collaborative working:

Get to know your colleagues. Understand what motivates, concerns, challenges or excites people, as this will help you to provide support and will encourage them to work together. This can be done in many ways – from organizing social events to simply paying attention to people.

Keep colleagues informed by asking what information would be most helpful, by openly sharing available information and by taking time to explain issues carefully. It also means providing information before it is requested and testing understanding to see where clarification is needed.

Put the interests of the business first. Identify an issue where you believe you can improve the situation and then work with others to do this.

Establish cross-business teams of managers (e.g. in specific areas such as marketing managers, finance managers, product managers). This group can meet either formally or informally to provide mutual support and discuss: recent successes, current priorities and challenges, and potential opportunities.

Arrange for team members to be seconded to other businesses. This will improve their skills and help to exchange expertise and best practice. Also, organize in-house training events and invite members from other teams.

Build a cross-functional team for a particular project. The following actions will go a long way to achieving this:

- Understand what you value in each member of the team – and tell them.
- Recognize where others can show their skills to best effect.
- Notice others in your team, or across the business, doing something right and praise them.
- Show support for the team as a whole – focusing on overall progress as well as individual contributions.
- Celebrate good performance.
- Promote the team to others.
- Praise others more than you criticize.
- Recognize the success of other teams across the business.
- Avoid setting expectations too high.

Find out where team members need support. You may not be able to solve the problem yourself, but help them find their own solutions by encouraging them to think creatively and by removing any constraints.

Encourage openness by being open yourself. Openness will help to draw people to you, leading them to understand and support your view and behave in a way that is reassuring and collegial. Openness is encouraged by setting a personal example and being candid. It also means listening to others without passing judgment, providing opportunities that encourage openness without being threatening, and boosting others' confidence. Take care to be your authentic self – any attempt to put on a front is easily seen through.

Review the way your team is remunerated. In most cases reward becomes an issue when people's perception of fairness is challenged. Often this occurs because they learn a colleague in a similar role is paid more or when they see similar roles at a different salary scale in the market. Ensure that people consistently understand how their performance is measured and how their reward is benchmarked.

'Walk the talk'. Get into the day-to-day rhythm of the business, observe/ listen to customer interactions and look out for where your team members need help and support. You may not be able to solve the problem yourself, but you should be able to help them find their own solutions, free their thinking and possibly remove constraints (such as bureaucracy).

Convey a sense of urgency and enthusiasm. Five valuable qualities of successful leaders include: self-confidence, energy, empathy, conviction and vision. These qualities are essential for motivating and engaging employees. When conveying a sense of urgency and enthusiasm – or assessing your leadership generally – it can help to measure yourself against these qualities. If any one of these is missing or lacking, then you may be an effective manager, but not a successful leader.

Focus on your own drive and determination. Drive is the essence of leadership, and to lead from the front, by example, means displaying drive and determination, setting the tone and encouraging others to follow. This will go a long way to motivating and engaging people.

Overcome the fear of risk. The conventional, controlling business approach to managing risk predominates. However, rather like viewing the glass as half-empty rather than half full, it is only one perception, and a fairly limited one. In business, prudence and conventional logic demands that although there may be an advantage to taking a risk and winning, the dangers of failure are so great that it is probably better either to do nothing, or else to minimize the risk as much as possible. This limited approach may occasionally be valid, but it is far from adequate on its own. It takes no account of the complex nature of risk. Certainly, insurance and prudence have their place, but they need not always be the default option in situations of uncertainty, or the best approach to take most of the time.

Unfortunately, organizations take the fun out of risk. It is seen as a necessary evil and suffers, as a result, from being perceived as bureaucratic and stifling – which frequently it is. Organizations fail to see that risk is both desirable, providing new opportunities to learn, develop and move forward, and necessary, compelling people to improve and meet the challenge of change.

An important point for leaders is to understand that waiting for someone to prove their trust does not work. The issue is not 'can I trust them' but 'I will trust them'. Trust is not only earned – it must be given. Remember that if you trust someone, they usually live up to it.

Also, you cannot create trust if you view it as a means to an end. If you cynically try to build trust, you are unlikely to succeed. It is people that care about building relationships for their own sake, who make and keep commitments and for whom honesty and integrity are important, that succeed in building trust. Several other points about trust are also worth noting:

• You cannot create trust without respected values. The values of integrity and honesty are the basis of all trusting relationships and high-trust cultures.
• Trust is often invisible or taken for granted. We can fail to realize that things are going well because of trust or badly because of the lack of it.

Whilst trust is often invisible it only exists as the result of constant actions and attention to the relationships and actions that create it. It is only when it disappears that we notice its absence. Its low profile status does not diminish its power. In fact, trust often only becomes visible when it has been lost or abused in some way.

• Trust requires commitment. Trust does not just happen. It requires commitment, personal responsibility and vigilance.

• Trust relies on reciprocal relationships. Trust centres around the virtuous cycle of 'giving and getting' interactions. Well-balanced people get psychological satisfaction from being trusted and as they are trusted more, so their trustworthiness grows.

Leaders can learn to extend trust by teaching them to set goals and boundaries, allow people freedom to work out how to achieve the goals, offer support combined with monitoring, and recognize and evaluate results.

• Trust opens up possibilities that can never exist without it. Without trust, people and organizations can never be totally efficient, creative and successful, because trust allows people to try new things, disagree with others and say what they want to say.

• Trust means understanding why people should (or do) respect you. This means understanding what your goal is in a particular situation and how you can work with people to achieve it. Of course, it also means behaving ethically by gathering the facts and understanding where the problems lie, thinking through the issues and considering the consequences of actions. Know your obligations and understand your own motives and feelings.

• Trust is time-sensitive and fragile and complex. For example, a firm may be trusted by its customers but despised by its employees, and think that the situation is fine. It is not. Trust and mistrust are like water, they flow, they get everywhere and they can be more powerful than they appear at first sight. Mistrust is especially corrosive so, for example, the firm will soon find that its problems with its workforce are inevitably being transmitted to its customers.

• Understand that the alternatives to (or substitutes for) trust are limited or non-existent. For example, understand that contracts and documents are no substitute for genuine trust. They may serve a purpose, but that is not creating trust and they can actually jeopardize it. The spirit of an agreement is often as important as the letter of the law.

Crucially, trust can take a long time to build and it can be destroyed in an instant. It can take much commitment, many actions and a long time to create trust – and only one small act to destroy it.

Use visioning to increase collaboration and understanding

'Visioning' means developing a coherent description of your business in the future. A clear, dynamic vision provides a clear focus for action, guiding people's decisions at all levels and helping to instill confidence and resolve. An essential element of visionary thinking is future orientation – the ability to communicate a clear view of the future of a business: its aims and what it is achieving. Future orienta-

It is often the case that, as managers, we tend to focus on managing for today but we are less effective at preparing for tomorrow. A defining role of a leader is their ability to set the right course and then take people with them.

tion applies to managers at all levels, whereas visionary thinking is most relevant to senior and mid-level managers. Visioning or visualization techniques can equally well be used at a personal level, to enable someone to get a clear focus on a personal development or behavioural change goal.

A clear, dynamic vision of the future succeeds by: inspiring and engaging people, unlocking energy and commitment; providing a clear focus for the future, guiding actions and decisions at all levels, and promoting confidence, determination and success.

Visioning can be usefully applied at several different levels:

Type of vision	Purpose and value	Characteristics
Overall vision for the organization (corporate vision)	Provides a clear direction and aspiration for the business Inspires, mobilizes and engages people Guides behaviour and decisions at all levels (providing a starting point for other business visions)	Inspiring and aspirational, clearly setting the direction, tone and priorities for the whole organization as well as informing customers and shareholders

Continued

Type of vision	Purpose and value	Characteristics
Vision for a business unit, department or team	Provides a clear, guiding direction for the business unit, department or team Supports the overall vision by translating it into a realistic aspiration for the smaller team, sustaining commitment and energy	Inspiring and directly relevant to the work of the team, it engages and mobilizes people so they work together, contributing to the overall success of the business
A vision of a specific task or outcome	Provides a clear focus for action in a specific area or for a particular task Used when delegating, or when forming or reforming a team	Guides the way that the task or role is approached, ensuring a clear view of what success will look like

(For further information see *Business Strategy* by Jeremy Kourdi, published by The Economist/Profile Books)

There is no single way to develop visionary thinking and future orientation; however, the following actions are designed to help you get started:

• Decide what you want – don't just accept what other people believe. Decide for yourself what will be important in the future.

• Trust your intuition. If you feel that a situation is changing and different, or if you have an idea that makes sense to you, explore it further.

• Test your assumptions and tap into the future. Insights do not readily come from old information, so look for trends and try to understand why things are changing, not just how.

• Get people to understand and support the vision by: communicating in an exciting and practical way; speaking positively so that people are intrigued, challenged and motivated; being honest and open; bringing the vision to life, ideally with examples; listening and acting on what people say, and encouraging people to see what the vision means for customers.

Finally, remember the characteristics of progressive views of the future – they are:

- Powerful. This has two parts: it must be imaginable and paint a clear picture of what the future will look like; it must also excite and inspire as many people as possible.
- Communicable. It must be possible for the vision to be communicated to anyone quickly and easily.
- Desirable and realistic. The vision needs to appeal to customers, employees and stakeholders.
- Focused. The vision needs to be specific and 'real-world' enough to guide decision-making.
- Adaptive. The vision needs to be general enough to accommodate individual initiatives, and flexible enough to allow for changing conditions.

Develop creativity and innovation

In her book *Hot Spots: Why Some Teams, Workplaces, and Organizations Buzz with Energy – and Others Don't* Professor Lynda Gratton highlights several important attributes of an innovative team. These include a cooperative mindset: people really have to want to share not only the explicit knowledge (which is relatively easy) but also the tacit knowledge which exists in people's heads. This mindset results from a company's practices, processes, behaviours and norms, and the behaviour of top management is a significant factor.

Boundary spanning is the opposite of the silo mentality where businesses or functions remain separate from each other, unconnected or even competitive. People who are good at spanning boundaries are vital for hotspots to succeed. Several specific skills and personal attributes are important including being undeterred by physical distance, welcoming a diverse range of ideas, insights, experience and people, and being willing and able to explore issues together. Starting as strangers is an advantage as the process of getting to know each other helps to build creativity and innovation. Also valuable is networking and building bridges for others. Boundary spanners are good at introducing people to others with whom valuable cooperation might develop. For example, strong ties between people who share a similar background, experience and emotional concerns mean that trust can be developed quickly. Weak ties, which use less time and emotion and may be more numerous, can be organized into new combinations to generate new insights. Finally, it helps to develop the art of constructive conversations. These are characterised by reflective listening, rather than emphasizing a particular point of view, as well as being willing to change or modify a view or perspective.

Developing a sense of purpose is another valuable technique that combines visioning and boundary spanning. It is best achieved by posing a challenging (or igniting) question. These questions do not possess a single 'right' answer; instead, they invite the exploration of a range of options, focused around a specific intention or issue. The value of these questions is that they can help find the best way to inspire and engage people. A questioning approach that leads to an exciting, igniting vision provides both purpose and energy.

Build a diverse team and empathic approach

Another aspect of heart leadership, this means encouraging collaboration between people, irrespective of their culture or walk of life. Diversity is enhanced by increasing exposure to other perspectives and ways of working, in order to stimulate new ideas and spark innovation and creativity. This can be accomplished by ensuring access, via recruitment, to diverse groups of potential employees (and thereby customers) and training all employees to be sensitive to the spoken and unspoken communications of people from different backgrounds.

Leading people from diverse cultures is another test of collaborative ability and one that requires empathy. Empathy helps the twenty-first-century leader travel effectively among different cultures. Empathic leaders possess a capacity to identify with the needs, values and beliefs of others in a way that communicates understanding and respect for other ways of living and working. Empathy and toughness are not mutually exclusive; empathy does not mean relaxing standards. It simply means putting yourself in another person's shoes so completely that you can feel what they are feeling. This goes beyond intellectual understanding of another's concerns and means taking action that communicates heartfelt understanding. Leaders must balance their inherent drive for performance with real empathy; they must be responsive to colleagues and customers with different values but also be responsible for achieving the objectives and representing the values of their organization, which may conflict sometimes with local country needs. Managing the paradox means setting limits on their empathy while not becoming hardened to local concerns.

Dealing with different cultures or groups is not about trying to copy or reject what you find different. Doing business and working across cultures and boundaries is very much about integrating the strength of one group or culture with that of another.

Using intellect, intelligence and insight

As we highlighted earlier, growing complexity, volatility and competition constantly demand new perspectives. Using your heart needs to be balanced with rational thinking: intellect, intelligence and insight. Crucially, it is not simply what we know that matters, but how we react to what we do not know.

Thinking about leading with your head prompts several useful techniques and skills, some of which may have become neglected. These include:

- rethinking and reframing;
- focusing on results and getting things done;
- developing and articulating a point of view.

Rethinking

Given the pace of change, the scope of new, unfamiliar and unpredictable challenges that leaders often face, and the competitive nature of business life, it can help immeasurably to increase one's capacity to rethink. Rethinking is an essential part of learning and developing new skills – and these have always been essential leadership qualities.

There are several reasons why many leaders are often predisposed to avoid rethinking. These include: pressure to produce results, lack of time to think, the rising cost of reinvention, and the inertia created by cultural rituals and norms. However, there are several ways that twenty-first-century leaders can increase their capacity in this area. First, analysing information and data is a great catalyst for producing a fresh viewpoint. Also, information – ranging from market trends to views of their personal behaviour – invariably prompts a focused, questioning and possibly even a reflective stance. This can then lead to informed dialogue and discussion.

We can break the frame of cultural tradition by, for example, taking people out of familiar environments and making them rely on new ideas and perspectives to solve complex business problems. Crucially, leaders must learn to pick the right times for rethinking – if they are continuously coming up with a new approach, it will make them look fickle or impulsive and their team will learn to filter out their latest ideas. Rethinking is a powerful tool that needs to be used carefully.

Reframing

Reframing is another valuable technique closely related to rethinking. Firm and definite boundaries are disappearing fast. This requires twenty-first-century leaders to reframe boundaries around their role, work and organization, and cope emotionally with the uncertainty of doing things in a new way.

Coping with moveable boundaries needs leaders to be aware of five different boundaries they must reframe:

- External boundaries – everything must now be judged by world class standards, not the company's performance last year.
- Vertical boundaries – leaders need to focus on their coaching and mentoring responsibilities and this requires greater transparency.
- Horizontal boundaries – peer influence and partnerships are crucial for getting things done.
- Geographical boundaries – globalization means working with unfamiliar cultures in a networked world.
- Personal boundaries – people must manage their idiosyncrasies and personal weaknesses in a more transparent, unforgiving environment.

With each of these boundaries the status quo is maintained by various barriers such as: incentive systems, corporate culture, arrogance, stress and lack of time. Getting leaders to adopt a reframing mindset involves raising their awareness that boundaries are changing and then, when they trip over a boundary, to intervene with coaching or leadership development.

Reframing is based on the view that if we see something one particular way then our actions respond accordingly. So, for example, if we view something as being threatening then we respond defensively. However, if we change our frame of reference by looking at the same situation from a different point of view, we can change and improve the way we respond.

Context reframing is based on the view that the meaning of a particular behaviour or event is tied to the context in which it occurs. Fundamentally, every action or behaviour is appropriate in some context. With a context reframe, a person takes the disliked behaviour and asks 'Where or when could this behaviour be useful?' or 'In what other context would this particular behaviour be of value?'

For example, I once knew a colleague whose work used to be a little slower than their contemporaries. The individual felt pressured and that was what their boss focused on. One day I pointed out that the quality of their work was superb – valued by customers and a standard for everyone else. My colleague wasn't slow or unproductive, they were meticulous and thorough. This subsequently had implications for the way they worked and the way the office was organized – my colleague met with clients and set the standard internally precisely because they were so expert.

Focusing on results and getting things done

Leaders who apply a combination of intellect, emotional intelligence and courage are better able to prioritize work, grasp the complexity of a task and understand the people issues and risk affecting execution. In practice, some leaders are brilliant strategists while others focus on operational issues, but they are rarely both. The essential challenge is to find a balance between knowing when to be operational and when to be strategic.

Getting things done in a chaotic, unforgiving environment requires leaders to use several simple tactics:

• Find the right balance between operational and strategic mindsets for you personally, working in your role. It can help leaders to solicit feedback from their colleagues on this issue.

- Develop influence through lateral relationships. The day when leaders control large teams in a hierarchical structure is disappearing. Influence without direct authority is often increasingly important for success.
- Create a climate of accountability. People need to know what is expected of them. Success needs to be recognized and shortcomings need to be addressed. There really is no substitute for a positive, dynamic approach – and sometimes this may require a tough conversation.

Organizations desperate for improved performance still often choose leaders who are seen as tough – but you don't get things done through force and fear.

- Develop perseverance. No one progresses smoothly through a career succeeding with everything first time; perseverance, including the ability to learn and improve, is essential. This applies to everyone, always, and is a particular hallmark of the most successful leaders.
- Focus on people's strengths rather than their weaknesses. Too many leaders, people management professionals and leadership development programmes concentrate on fixing weaknesses, when what works better is maximizing strengths. Of course, some skills need to be brought up to a minimum acceptable standard but the point is that we can all find things we can say we are good at: what we need to be doing is capitalizing on what we are good at to achieve a common goal.

Developing and articulating a point of view

A viewpoint is simply an overarching, strongly-held system of beliefs that apply to everything from individual behaviour to values to business strategy. It provides an internal sense of security and a base from which decisions can be made in a sometimes political, complex and unclear corporate environment. It helps leaders generate commitment and motivation and maintain a consistent, credible image. Articulating the point of view is also a valuable step in developing or shifting an organization's culture.

Leaders sometimes fail to develop a point of view because of a mistaken notion that confuses loyalty to the organization with furthering its goals – and they might indeed rely on critical questioning. The organization may encourage adherence to one specific way of working, or there may simply be a failure to investigate and think about the outside world.

To overcome such obstacles and to help people develop a point of view several steps are important. First, define the challenge. It is important to be clear about the issues and their implications. Next, gather useful and compelling information that both supports your point of view as well as information that may support the status quo. This will help with the next stage which is to converge the ideas into a single viewpoint. To do this, consider: what are the failings of the existing approach? Why is your point of view preferable? Next, test the idea with others, listening carefully, and finally reconfigure and refine your viewpoint.

Courageous leadership

Guts leadership is not about being tough and aggressive. It is about doing the right thing based on the context, although it is important to take care this does not turn into self-righteousness, narrow-mindedness or misplaced stubbornness. Courageous leadership has several important elements:

* taking risks with incomplete data;
* acting with unyielding integrity;
* balancing risk and reward;
* communicating in the right way and at the right time.

Taking risks with incomplete data

Leadership courage is often a matter of vision and values, knowing what to believe and when to act according to those beliefs. This means making decisions that involve some risk, based on beliefs and instinct, rather than relying exclusively on the data. It is not a matter of ignoring the facts. Sometimes there is no time to assemble all the facts, sometimes the data are ambiguous, and sometimes there is information overload. In some situations, leaders need to use their intuition combined with whatever facts exist to arrive at more effective decisions.

Leaders can be encouraged to rely on their instincts as well as the data by connecting with new contacts as well as people at the margins (e.g. young people, new hires) who ignore traditional practices. Coaching is also valuable as it can help leaders to uncover the assumptions underlying their decisions. Finally, getting out of the office and into the world of customers, suppliers and other outsiders is a great way to gain a new perspective and clarity of view.

Balancing risk and reward

When making decisions in a complex world, twenty-first-century leaders must balance short-term risk with longer-term rewards and determine how much pressure they can withstand from those who must endure short-term sacrifices. Balancing risk and reward and coping with the uncertainty between the two requires more courage than ever. Some leaders take foolish chances with catastrophic financial consequences; others are overly cautious, refuse to take appropriate risk, and deprive their organizations of significant reward.

Balancing risk truly is an area where intellect, emotion and courage need to combine. The best leaders have a sense of when to push, and how far is too far. They don't just possess courage: they temper their courage with their head and heart.

In recent years, several factors have broadened, intensified and complicated risk. This includes the stock market's unrelenting emphasis on performance and growth, the need to enter less stable or well-known emerging markets, increasing regulatory scrutiny, interdependence of companies, technological change, and the growing importance of knowledge and intangibles. As if that wasn't enough, there are now many different categories of risk – personal, reputational, structural. As a result, there is no standard or uniform formula for dealing with risk and reward.

Leaders should aim to create a climate in which they can balance difficult, paradoxical situations. This means giving them the opportunity to reflect on the balance and develop the courage needed to maintain that balance, rather than turn conservative and avoid any risk at the first hint of trouble. This can be achieved by explaining openly about risk and reward decisions, as well as coaching leaders to encourage greater self-awareness and making them aware of their derailing behaviours (the most likely derailer being excessive caution).

Acting with unyielding integrity

The most important part of leading with guts is character – knowing what you stand for and what you are willing to stand up for. This means having a set of values that underpin your actions. Values need to be transparent and inspiring to others. It is simultaneously both more difficult and more necessary than ever before for leaders to act with unyielding integrity. However, integrity is not a black-or-white issue; it is not necessarily a question of choosing between a clearly right or a clearly wrong course of action. Most people who violate their integrity don't realize they're doing it – caught up in the need to act or a desire to achieve a challenging goal, they can do things that they realize with hindsight were mistakes.

So, can integrity be developed? Our view is that values and integrity are formed well before one enters the workplace, and they should be brought into the workplace. However, integrity at work benefits from a process of building and displaying character. It is important to note that this is not a question of ignoring political considerations. The best leaders pick their moments and establish reputations for acting according to a consistent set of values. Integrity emerges (or fails to emerge) during extraordinary, defining moments. The key to succeeding with integrity is to be self-aware and clear about what you hold to be most important. This awareness can be fostered by facilitating reflection and discussion about integrity issues, encouraging people to articulate what they are thinking of doing before they do it, and asking thought-provoking questions to help people determine what they believe and value.

Communicating

If you doubt the power of communication in the twenty-first century consider this: one reason Barack Obama is so popular is because he appeals to our emotions and aspirations with his personality, powerfully conveyed through his words. And one reason why most politicians are so unpopular is because they do not.

It has become normal for words and expressions to become ubiquitous and devalued. People believe that communication is easy, when the opposite is true. If anything, communication is at a premium for two reasons. First, the way words are used and the results they achieve remain vital for progress and success. This applies anywhere, in any language. Second, words are amplified through modern technology, spreading further, faster. They are more immediate and influential than ever. Despite this, the skills of communication risk being lost or forgotten.

Great communications from leaders have several characteristics. Understanding these can help explain why there are (or appear to be) fewer great speakers around today. First, the best speakers are not afraid to be open and personal or to show their passion and values. This builds trust and a connection, and it means listeners get to know the speaker. For example, Sebastian Coe opened his presentation for London's bid to host the 2012 Olympics with a very personal, engaging story. He spoke about how he watched a black and white television in his school to see two local athletes competing at the 1968 Olympics. He spoke movingly: 'That day a window to a new world opened for me. By the time I was back in my classroom, I knew what I wanted to do and what I wanted to be'.

Those leaders who communicate best also show empathy, understand their audience and appeal to their values. This is valuable for any speaker: who is your audience? What are your mutual interests? For example, Winston Churchill understood that people wanted a confident, defiant, resolute leader – a sense of clarity and purpose.

Virtues of honesty, fairness and courage are also hallmarks of a great leader and these also need to be powerfully expressed. Typically, we want them for ourselves and we value them in others. Also, leaders let their words suit the moment and this often means being clear, determined and unequivocal. Great speakers think about their message and how to engage their audience.

Perhaps the reason that there are so few great speakers around today (notably in corporate life but also in other areas such as politics) is that mastering the complexity of modern communications has come to dominate at the expense of traditional values and virtues. For example, Tony Blair and Bill Clinton are great communicators but they are both criticized for values that are seen as skin-deep. Gordon Brown, in contrast, is recognized for his 'moral compass' but widely seen as a weak communicator with limited influence. Speakers need to master the message and the media, and this double challenge proves difficult for many. Also, people seem to be more reticent than in the past about giving of themselves when speaking publicly, perhaps for fear of criticism or ridicule.

Finally, it may just be the case that the reason leaders fail to engage with their people is because there are fewer leaders who genuinely hold universal values that connect with others. For example, after the corporate scandals, malfeasance and excesses of the 2000s can we really say that politicians and executives understand their leadership role? Do they understand their influence and the expectations of their constituents? I suspect the answer is no – or not completely. In those areas where universal qualities of courage and service remain, for example the military, then great communication persists from people like General David Petraeus and General Sir Mike Jackson. What works well everywhere is a clear realization of what people value – understand that, and you begin to become an engaging, courageous communicator.

Empowering people

Empowerment is based on the belief that an individual's abilities are frequently under-used and, given the right work environment and level of responsibility, people will start to make a much greater, positive contribution. When empowering team members you are letting them get on with the job entirely: they are both responsible and accountable, within certain agreed boundaries. Empowerment means: letting each member of the team get on with their job; letting those team members closest to customers take decisions; removing obstacles and unnecessary bureaucracy, and encouraging and enabling people to put their ideas for improvement into practice.

Empowerment requires the leader to:

- Set a clear, unambiguous direction and ensure that people remain on course.
- Retain a full understanding of what is happening.
- Offer support, open doors, and clear the way for action without taking over from those delegated to do the job.
- Make decisions which others cannot, either because of lack of time, information or knowledge.
- Continuously assess performance, reward progress, and support individual and team development.

- Build trust through shared success and share information and knowledge whenever it is possible to do so.

Inviting feedback is a great way of showing openness and trust as well as inspiring trust in return. Feedback is useful, and inviting it means knowing what subjects you want people to comment on – and why. It is vital to avoid becoming defensive or arguing with the comments; instead, reflect on feedback carefully and decide whether to act.

How well (and how often) do you do this? Several principles will help you as a leader to empower members of your team. First, understand what you mean by empowerment. Make sure you know what you want to get out of empowering your team; let your colleagues and senior managers know your plans, and check that their expectations meet your own. Next, assess the barriers to empowerment – what are they (for example, people may fear responsibility or there may be a culture of blame), and how can they be overcome?

It is also important to build the right culture within your team – some organizations have cultures that are more conducive to empowerment than others. If you are serious about empowering your team to make their own decisions and take greater responsibility then you should promote trust and respect; remove a climate of fear and blame, and focus on the needs of the task, team and each individual.

Next, establish the right boundaries – empowerment provides people with greater autonomy and responsibility but it is vital to agree and set clear limits. This may include, for example, agreeing expenditure limits. Also, be prepared to have these boundaries tested: only then will clear limits be established. You will need to raise awareness among those around you of what is involved in empowerment: this may involve reassuring some, selling the benefits and winning the support of others.

Make sure that people have the right skills and resources to take control – review what each member of your team does now and what they are likely to be doing in future. This is an opportunity to alter and update job descriptions; assess training needs, and make sure that your team has sufficient resources.

Agree objectives and performance measures and then monitor progress. Empowerment is about giving people the responsibility and resources to complete their tasks. As with delegation, it is not about dumping work on people and leaving them, and it requires you to agree the necessary level of speed, accuracy and cost-efficiency. You will also need to make people aware of what is happening and try to secure early 'wins' that highlight the value of the process. Monitor developments and iron out any difficulties, particularly in the early days, but take care not to interfere or undermine the process.

It is important to understand that when you empower your team members you are giving them a complete job and area of responsibility, within definite boundaries, rather than delegating one specific task or project.

Coaching and developing talent

Coaching is a vital skill that you can learn and employ in your everyday practice. It helps people succeed with challenges, opportunities and the unexpected or unfamiliar. It is also very rewarding: it helps individuals to develop their skills, achieve their potential and succeed. Coaching enables individuals to step back from their day-to-day pressures with the dedicated support of a skilled professional. So, what are the elements of a good coaching conversation?

First, is the need for the coaching to be non-directive and non-judgmental. Great coaches are positive, constructive and 'on your side'. Coaches also take control and are given control. This means they are able to provide clarity, focus, reassurance; they challenge and provoke people; they can be directive and, above all, they stimulate and get through to people.

Another vital aspect of coaching is the ability to *question*. This works by showing interest, providing a feeling of support and building rapport. Thoughtful questioning also uncovers, explores and builds on issues, goals, options, realities, ideas and potential changes, and it enables people to think about issues in a different way.

Discussing and reframing issues is another skill of great coaches as it provides a valuable new perspective. Simply saying or hearing an issue described can provide people with a new perspective. Also, good coaching *challenges basic assumptions*. Do this by encouraging people to find ideas and a way forward by: removing constraints, highlighting new opportunities, and providing a different way of thinking and a different reality to the one originally perceived. Coaches also *use models and techniques* and this means they are looking for new ideas and keen to develop their skills. Models and techniques provide energy, focus and a new perspective.

A good coaching conversation should summarize, reframe and help the individual set goals for the future. Schedule a series of conversations to keep in touch with these goals. It is important to recognize that each individual needs to 'buy-in' to the process, so help colleagues understand the technique you are using and give them the space to question you in return. A successful coaching conversation builds insight and enthusiasm for change and can help individuals understand how they are performing and reach decisions on their careers.

Inspiring Trust

- Do people tend to open up to you and tell you things about themselves that they don't tell many others?
- Are you generally accepting and non-judgmental of others?
- Do you offer your help and support? When – and how could this improve?
- Do you make sure that people feel comfortable around you?
- Do you readily admit when you are wrong or have made a mistake (and apologize when necessary)?
- Do you give credit readily and effectively for things that others have done?
- Do you communicate in an open, honest and genuine way?
- Do you try to understand other people's intentions instead of judging them just on their actions?
- Are you genuinely interested in people or do you try and fake it? (If so, they will almost certainly know.)
- Do you give others a chance to have their say and do you genuinely listen to them?

Building Trusted Relationships

Several practical actions will help you to build trusted relationships:

- Deliver what you say you will, and be true to your word.
- Create an expectation of trust, by trusting others.
- Keep team members informed by asking what information would be most helpful, explaining issues carefully and sharing available information.
- Give constructive feedback by clearly identifying the behaviour that you are giving feedback on (focus on the behaviour, not the person).

More generally, make sure you:

- Treat each individual with respect and offer support.
- Illustrate comments with practical examples.
- Agree a plan of action and stick with it.
- Make sure your comments are constructive.
- Act with integrity and sincerity.
- Treat others as you would wish to be treated yourself.
- Understand who you are dealing with, taking time to find out how they work and what motivates them.
- Be dutiful, diligent and consistent.
- Recognize success and reward good performance.

Using Coaching

The GROW Model

The GROW model, developed by Sir John Whitmore, provides a framework for coaching.* GROW is an acronym with four stages:

Continued

---

*For further information about the GROW model see *Coaching for Performance* by John Whitmore, Nicholas Brealey Publishing. For a practical guide to this subject see *Coaching Essentials – Practical, proven techniques for world-class executive coaching* by Patricia Bossons, Jeremy Kourdi and Denis Sartain, published by A&C Black.

- Goals.
- Reality.
- Options.
- Will / When.

Each stage provides a guide to a vital part of the coaching conversation and while it is usually taken in sequence it is not necessarily a linear process – coaches can move between stages when needed.

Goals. This stage focuses on the coachee's goals: their aims and priorities. It sets the agenda for the coaching conversation. During this stage the coach should be flexible and prepared to explore, question and challenge. This is achieved with questioning and empathy. The outcome of this stage is a clear set of goals both for the overall coaching relationship and, in particular, for that coaching session. Questions at this stage include:

- What is your goal? What are your priorities? What are you trying to achieve?
- How will you know when you have achieved it?
- Would you define it as an end goal (e.g. set up a new team) or a performance goal (get the existing team to be more collaborative)?
- If it is an end goal, what performance goal could be related to it?
- Is the goal specific and measurable?
- How will you know when it has been achieved? What will success look like?

Reality. The next step is exploring the learner's current position: the reality of their circumstances and their concerns relating to their specific goal. The coach needs to help the coachee quickly analyse and understand the most significant issues relating to their goal. This can include facts or figures, obstacles, resources or people involved. The coach helps the coachee understand the reality of their situation by asking questions that uncover the reality. The coach can also help by providing information, if possible, and also by summarizing the situation to help to clarify the reality for the coachee. Questions at this stage include:

- To what extent can you control the result? What sort of things won't you have control over?
- Do you feel that achieving the goal will stretch or break you?

- When do you want to achieve the goal by? How feasible is this?
- What are the milestones or key points on the way to achieving your goal?
- Who is involved and what effect could they have on the situation?
- What have you done about this situation so far, and what have been the results?
- What are the major constraints or issues you are (or may be) faced with?
- Are these constraints major or minor? How could their effect be reduced?
- What other issues are occurring at work that might have a bearing on your goal?

Options. During this stage of the process the coach helps the coachee to generate options, strategies and action plans for achieving their goal. Sometimes, this discussion can continue to uncover new aspects of the individual's current position, with the result that discussion reverts back to the coachee's reality. This is fine if it is productive or enlightening – the aim is to help the individual, not to rigidly follow a process. Questions at this stage include:

- What options do you have?
- Which options do you favour and why?
- If you had unlimited resources, what options would you have?
- Could you link your goal to some other organizational issue – would this generate new options?
- What would be the perfect solution?

Will / When. The final stage is vital yet often neglected or rushed. The aim is to clearly agree what needs to be done; what action will be taken, by whom, how and when, and to ensure that sufficient will, commitment and determination is present to see this through.

It can help for the coachee to develop a practical plan to implement their chosen option. The coach's role is to provide a sounding board, highlighting strengths and weaknesses, testing the approach and offering an additional perspective that supports the coachee. Questions at this stage include:

- What are you going to do?
- When are you going to do it?
- Who needs to know?

Continued

- What support and resources do you need and how will you get them?
- How will the above help you to achieve your goals?
- What obstacles might hinder you and how will you overcome these?
- How will you ensure success?

Often, the most effective plans also incorporate a review and feedback process. This is valuable for checking progress and providing the necessary resources and will.

Conclusion
Creating a Talent Flywheel

Our aim in writing this book has been to highlight where talent management thinking is limited and propose a more effective alternative. Our first hand experience and research tells us that an alternative is overdue. Our organizations require an approach that is simple and competitive. Our colleagues need this to be compelling. We can no longer operate in the belief that talent is an absolute quality that applies strictly to the most able individuals. Nor can we continue to think about talent as something that the organization controls and manages. The world has moved on.

The world we now live in demands much more of us. This is changing the way we need to work and how we choose to shape our careers. The 'Capability Crunch' is the biggest threat to our competitiveness and organizations must act to reach the potential of all their people. This isn't about training it's about engaging. This means being resolutely clear about the purpose of your organization; why it exists and how it will make a difference. It also involves organizing work in ways that allow people to 'dial up and down' to balance personal commitments. We must also realize that humans need work to be stimulating. We love to learn, we relish solving things and we are built to be creative. We guarantee that the absence of stimulating work will dry up your talent supply.

Perhaps the most fundamental conclusion we have drawn from our research is the importance of belief in the talent debate. This relates to the mental model you have about talent, where you look for it and how you engage with it. We talked in our introduction about the 'Talent Doom Loop', how we have tried to tackle the talent problem through a series of disconnected or localized interventions.

We have illustrated how the old hierarchies and ideas about control are breaking down. We have also demonstrated that accessing talent is not about solely concentrating on brilliant individuals; it's about how you can create a brilliant mix of performances throughout your workforce. This requires a change in perspective. One that views the problem systemically, understanding that talent is essentially a social issue. It relates to the culture, behaviour and focus of an organization; the 'between employee factors' or social capital that utilizes the potential of the entire workforce.

The positive opposite of the 'Doom Loop' is the 'Fly Wheel'. The 'Fly Wheel' is based on a set of conditions, which when applied together in small, incremental steps create an irresistible momentum for change. The key here is to work on the problem in a joined up way so that each change reinforces

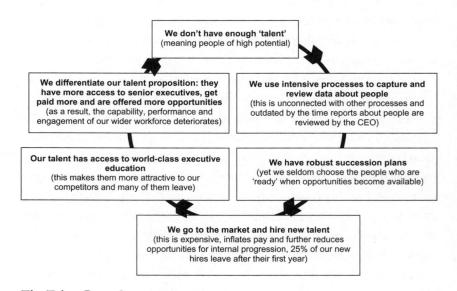

The Talent Doom Loop

another in a related part of the organization. The goal of the Talent Fly Wheel is to leverage the latent talents available to the organization; making the resulting whole much greater than the sum of its parts.

This is the most important truth about talent and our recommended conditions for the Talent Fly Wheel are summarized below.

See talent in context

First, think about talent in your context. Consider the demand and supply. What type of skills will your organization need to survive and thrive into the future? When will you need them and for how long? Play out a range of scenarios and set out a 'Make and Buy' plan. If you need the familiarity of succession plans, remember that they are risk management tools that date quickly.

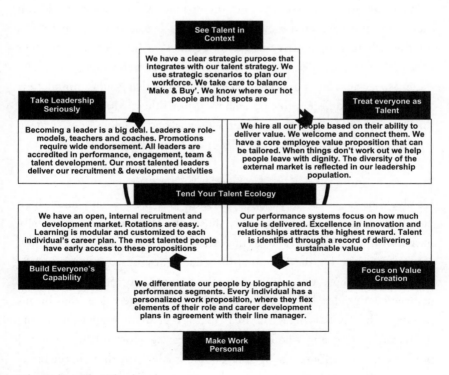

The Talent Fly Wheel

Think instead about the people and organization you need to deliver your strategy. How will your organization be more distinctive, efficient and innovative? Look at how people are performing today and *who* they are performing with. Understand what drives them and how a competitor might view them. This is not just about talent loving talented company; it's about talented teams; knowing where your hot people and 'hotspots' are (Gratton, 2007) *and* knowing how to replicate them.

Treat everyone as talent

We need a more sustainable perspective on our people. We are exhausting (metaphorically and literally) the seam of usual suspects and we must widen our search to different groups. We'll know we've made in-roads when we have more diverse representation at every leadership level. This will balance the portfolio of capabilities in the organization, making it more innovative and more adaptable.

We've got to also re-connect with the 'B-players' or as we prefer to call them the vital core of the organization. This means moving on from a mindset where people arrive at 'career ceilings' or 'they've reached their potential'. Yes, they might have stalled or be under-performing – so move them! Move them on a personal level towards work that is more stimulating. Move them to a different role or team to inspire others. Move them on with thanks out of the organization. Treating everyone as talent doesn't mean continuing to carry those whose skills or attitude no longer fit.

Focus on value creation

It's also time to move away from the notion that talent is only about high potentials. It is important to identify those who learn fast and continually outperform their peers. It's more important to be clear about the potential you need, answering the 'potential for what?' question. Our research tells us that increasingly this is not about the potential to reach more senior management grades. It's about the potential to generate value. This means making a differential impact in areas that are of the highest value to the organization. This might be in a technical area; e.g. more reliable actuarial prediction; in a customer facing area, doubling sales growth; or in the back-office, halving spend through new purchasing arrangements.

Whatever the context it's about finding the 'Animateurs', the people who bring change to life and create focus and energy in their work colleagues. This is not about skilled predictions of what people might (or might not) achieve into the future. It's about looking at their results today and how these will impact on the future of the organization.

Make work personal

People choose when and how they apply their talent. It's not simply a matter of assuming that an individual's ability belongs to the organization that pays them. Potential is a currency of exchange in today's workplace. It is shared when there is belief in the organization's purpose and trust in its leaders. It's also dependent on the degree of meaning an individual achieves through their work and this varies from person to person and at different times in their life.

We need to organize work differently to accommodate this. This goes beyond flexible working arrangements to the way we define roles and how we allow people to dial up and down on their responsibilities dependent on what's happening in the rest of their life.

This is terrifically complicated and requires a much more sophisticated HR strategy. We will need to employ market segmentation techniques to understand and respond to the different drivers of different groups. This will also require clarity on the Employee Value Proposition and how this can be customized on a personal level.

Build everyone's capability

We believe one of the key reasons we don't have enough talent is because education has not kept pace with the future. This has happened in our schools and universities. It has also happened in our workplaces. Part of the problem here is that employers have been focused on bridging the skill gap of those entering the workforce. This has created an education drift inside the learning and development function. At one end the priority is training, basic skills and job competencies; at the other end, expensive executive education; somewhere in the middle, mediocre management education.

The problem here is how the organization's curriculum stays relevant to its strategy and how employees can build their capabilities, as they need it.

Learning must become more convenient, continuous and customized. Segmentation will allow us to shape and target learning propositions more effectively. The most able must receive earlier (not exclusive) access to this education.

We must also move away from an over-reliance on content rich workshops or e-learning towards more varied experiences. Rotations, secondments, network membership and leadership of expert communities are increasingly important for talent development and for the organization's health. They also cost less and get better results than conventional activity.

We must also move from the idea of overly regimented training or the more current, self-directed (i.e. left to your own devices) learning and adopt an educative mindset. The original definition of education meant 'to draw out', quite literally to bring an individual's potential to life. To do this well, the organization needs its leaders to take on the role of teachers.

Take leadership seriously

A talented organization needs leaders in many guises. Thought leaders, customer champions, change agents, entrepreneurs and people leaders. They may be deep specialists in each of these areas or people who can combine the set. What matters is that performance standards are established around what it means to be a leader and that exemplary performance is recognized and celebrated.

Arguably people leadership is the most influential of the set, and this requires serious attention. It's interesting that what's perceived as the more sophisticated end of leadership, coaching, inspiring, engaging people, is normally left until relatively late on in a leader's career. We believe the role of a leader is so important to talent (and the organization) that it needs to be accredited and reviewed on a regular basis.

Tend your talent ecology

The Fly Wheel depends on the interaction of each of the above conditions with the organization's talent ecology. This is the complex set of relationships between individuals, teams, the external market, the organization's culture, its strategy, structure and operating habits. When aligned these elements form the final, powerful turn of the Fly Wheel and drive its momentum. They are the hardest to achieve and the easiest to lose.

On this final point and by way of warning, we are reminded of an important story about how this can go disastrously wrong. In the original *War for Talent*, the writers pointed to Enron as a shining example of a company on top of its game where talent was concerned. It focused on high potentials, it had an open internal labour market and it developed its talent to 'think outside the box'. What Enron's talent may have lacked however, was a sense of integrity and ability to challenge the status quo. Many have commented since that without these values to anchor their talent strategy Enron ran away with itself. It had enough talent, they could think outside of the box, but nobody stopped to ask whether it was the box itself that needed changing ...

Appendix: Researching the Truth About Talent

We received 302 responses to our survey. Participants were mainly women, 57% compared with 43% men. They also reflected a Generation X bias, with 44% between 35 and 44 years old, 19% between 25 and 34 years old. Twenty-eight per cent were Boomers, 45–54 years old, another 6% were over 55. Only 2% were under 25 years.

The majority of our participants (80%) were employed full time with the remaining group self-employed, working flexibly or on a career break. Sixty-one per cent have been working for at least 15 years.

They are above averagely qualified, 41% are graduates, 46% Masters graduates and 5% PhD students. Unsurprisingly, this also played out in income terms; over 50% earned between £70 and 150k equivalent.

Participants were mainly based in the UK (68%) or the US (12%), however, the remainder reached across all the continents: Europe, South America, Asia, the Middle East and Africa.

Professionally, 51% are HR professionals with a further 21% operating in consulting. The majority work in the financial services sector, 43% and remainder are distributed across a range of technical/professional areas: sales, marketing, accountancy, advertizing and education. Interestingly, 5% were from not-for-profit organizations.

As a group our participants said their most important work drivers were to: 'Stave Off Boredom, Travel and Make New Friends'. They were also most attracted to employers who offer: 'Stimulating Work, Inspiring Line Managers and Strong Corporate Values'.

The participant group were in strong agreement about the definition of talent. The majority identified talent as: 'high performers, strong leaders, innovators and those who were outstanding compared to their peers'. They described talent as people who build relationships, change things and invent things (in that order). These were viewed as the strongest indicators of value. Additionally, 'Insight, Passion and Vision' were identified as the most important qualities for talent. Importantly, the largest majority indicated that 'everyone had the potential to become more talented'.

The group believed that individual genetics continued to play an important part in talent. There was a comparative response rate on the importance of environmental factors. Of these an open and innovative culture was seen as most important for growing talent, with inspiring line managers, time for development and accessible executives also cited as essential.

The group believed that growing talent was equally the responsibility of senior executives, HR, line managers and individuals. Current performance against this responsibility was seen to be lacking, with all needing to do more. Almost 18% of respondents felt that HR was too invisible.

Research Acknowledgements

We are indebted to the experience and insights provided by our colleagues past and present. It is always invidious to single people out but we would particularly like to acknowledge those who have encouraged and inspired us along the way; Lisa Earnhardt, Rosemary D'arcy, Stephen Barrow, Barbara Simpson, Emma Mitchell, Ben Dunn, Catherine Phillips, Michelle Martin, Steve Mostyn, June Boyle, Claire Roberts, Ian Mackenzie, Ali Herdman, Ann Kleinsteuber, Andrew Mayo and Ben Summerskill.

We were fortunate to have over 300 people across the globe contribute to our research and their input gave us confidence that the talent agenda really did need to change. Thanks to each of you for your time and insight. We have listed those who were happy to be acknowledged in the research summary at the end of the book. We are also indebted to the London Goddess network who allowed us to digest the research findings over dinner – fortunately there we no reports of indigestion.

Thanks also to the patient team at Wiley for their commitment to this project.

We owe the biggest thanks to our friends and families who believed in us and enabled us to put our life on hold in order to let the book take shape. Thank you.

Finally to our respective partners Tania and Julie who sit in the shade behind the cover but who worked alongside us with every word that we typed. Thank you for the proof reading, the permission chasing, the kettle boiling and supporting us through the ups and downs. We couldn't have got this far without you.

1. Dr Raymond Madden Director, Corporate Leadership and Learning.
2. Cass Business School.
3. Jim Francis, Founder of Wavemaker Consulting.
4. Richard Colgan, Chief Executive, Oakleaf Partnership Limited.
5. Johan Ludike, MTN Group Limited South Africa.
6. Simon Hayward.
7. John Arnott, HR Director, Vaultex.
8. Amelia Hughes, Independent Business Psychologist.

9. Dr. Piet-Hein Prince MBA, CISA. Ernst & Young Advisory Services.
10. Lara Fascione.
11. Nicola Shearer, Director Little Spring time.
12. Keith Robson, Barclays.
13. Frances Middleton.
14. Lenore Beilings, South Africa.
15. Peter Simpson, Bristol Business School.
16. James Taylor, HSBC.
17. Barbara Simpson, Cancer Research UK.
18. Allie Kerevan.
19. Tim Hopgood, Lloyds Banking Group.
20. Neil Lawson, Director – Marton House plc.
21. Lizzie Holden, Director The Global Coaching House.
22. Shona Marshall, The Miller Group.
23. Philippe Husser.
24. Nick Warren, Performance Unlimited.
25. Jayne O'Hara, Oliver Wyman, Leadership Development.
26. Dimitra Manis, SVP – Global Head of Talent, Thomson Reuters.
27. Martyn Fricker, Director, Business Development, Emida Inc.
28. Marc Grainger, Credit Suisse.
29. Nikki Squelch, Scope.
30. Tariq Ahmed, Visa Inc.
31. Andy Nicoll.
32. Lillian Latto, Head of Research, Executive Search and Selection, Burns Carlton.
33. Craig McLoughlin, Director, magnum training ltd.
34. Marc Hoodless, Managing Director Human Resources, Arqaam Capital, Dubai.
35. Diane Yates, Director, Wyse People Development.
36. Lynn S. O'Connor.
37. Jacqueline Planner.
38. Brian D. Cawley, Ph.D. Corvirtus, LLC (Colorado Springs, CO USA).
39. Sarah Law, C.Psychol, Meercat Consulting Ltd.
40. Karin Wills.

41. Chris Locke, Head of Leadership Learning & Development, Pearson International.
42. Rachel James.
43. Ettie McCormack, owner of STEP Forward Solutions Ltd.
44. Mike Fitzgerald, Celent.
45. Shari Casey, Betfair.com.
46. Josephine Storek, Head of Corporate Relations EDHEC Business School UK.
47. James Gamage.
48. Ann Kleinsteuber.
49. Sally Bibb, Co-founder and Director of talentsmoothie.
50. Liz Grant, Director, Black Toucan.
51. Tim O'Rourke, Managing Consultant at Woodcote HR Ltd.
52. Claire Roberts, Oliver Wyman.
53. Viv Taylor, Director of Organizational Development, Guardian News and Media.
54. Susan Chew.
55. Jeremy J. Lewis.
56. Russell Butler, CEO & Founder, iVentiv Ltd.
57. Tanja Riechel, Leadership Talent Management Consultant, MTN Group.
58. Simon Rodgers.
59. Lorraine Poole.
60. Anna Penfold, Korn/Ferry | Whitehead Mann.
61. Dr. Dena Michelli, Executive Coach.
62. Preya Gopie, Barclays.
63. Daryl Murray, Assessment Design Director, Penna plc.
64. Kay Rolandi MSc, FCIPD.
65. European Learning & Development Manager, Parker Hannifin Ltd.
66. John Drysdale, Director, Business Momentum.
67. Sean Miller MCIPD.
68. Peter Little, Senior HR Business Partner, Lloyds Banking Group.
69. Alison Verheul Crucible Consulting.
70. Jim Thornhill.
71. Matt Lowry.

Index